The Y
and
Scarborough
Railway.

by C. T. Goode.

Cover Picture: Domed ex 0.6.0 leaving Malton on an excursion for Whitby or Scarborough. There are seven coaches, several with clerestory roofs.

ISBN 1 870313 19 4
72 Woodland Drive, Anlaby, Hull. HU10 7HX

Burstwick Print & Publicity Services
13a Anlaby Road, Hull. HU1 2PJ

Foreword

Here is a railway which has all the ingredients for survival, with two large and healthy centres, one at each end, linked by train services which are modern, efficient and useful to a wide swathe of the community on each side. What happened to the intermediate stations could have happened anywhere, since these were opened on spec. in the hope that development in housing would take place, or that a tide of industry would arrive. As in many other parts of the country, however, nothing materialised and the wayside stations floundered, rather earlier than most in this case. One wonders whether Haxby and Strensall are due for a revival, as there is new housing appearing in the district. Still, time will tell.

In my enthusiast days I never actually travelled on this particular line much, simply because it was not included on a runabout ticket. Folk from my neck of the woods could reach Scarborough via Bridlington and Bubwith, or go round via Hull. I did travel that way once or twice, slowly up to Malton with frequent halts including one place with a strange nameboard which put me in mind of Uncle Remus and slavery. Huttonsambo? This bothered me for ages until I met Latin at school and realised that Ambo was the NER way of impressing the customers with its knowledge of the word for 'both' in that language.

Mention is made of the B16s, a wheezy lot. Books cannot produce sounds or smells, a pity where a railway is concerned, and the wailing note of one of these workhorses as it found its feet again after a check was most distinctive. Steam would completely obscure the front end and a driver's view forward. To a discerning boy it was obvious that NER engines wailed and wheezed, whereas GN and GC machines never did - something to do with tighter joints, I suppose.

My thanks to the library staff of the National Railway Museum, North Road Museum in Darlington and at York, Hull and Scarborough.

Acknowledgement is made to the Regional Railway History of Great Britain, works by the late Cecil J. Allen and a more recent one by Bill Fawcett on the same subject. Photographs used are from the Ken Hoole Collection on pages, 10, 11, 17, 19, 21, 22, 25, 28, 30, 32. Lens of Sutton 9, 13, 14, 16, 20, 33, 35. M. Black 37. J.W. Armstrong 12, 23, 27, 31, 38, 39, 41. T. Rounthwaite Front Cover, and the Author, whose transparencies, found at the last minute, appear finally.

C.T. Goode.
Anlaby 1998.

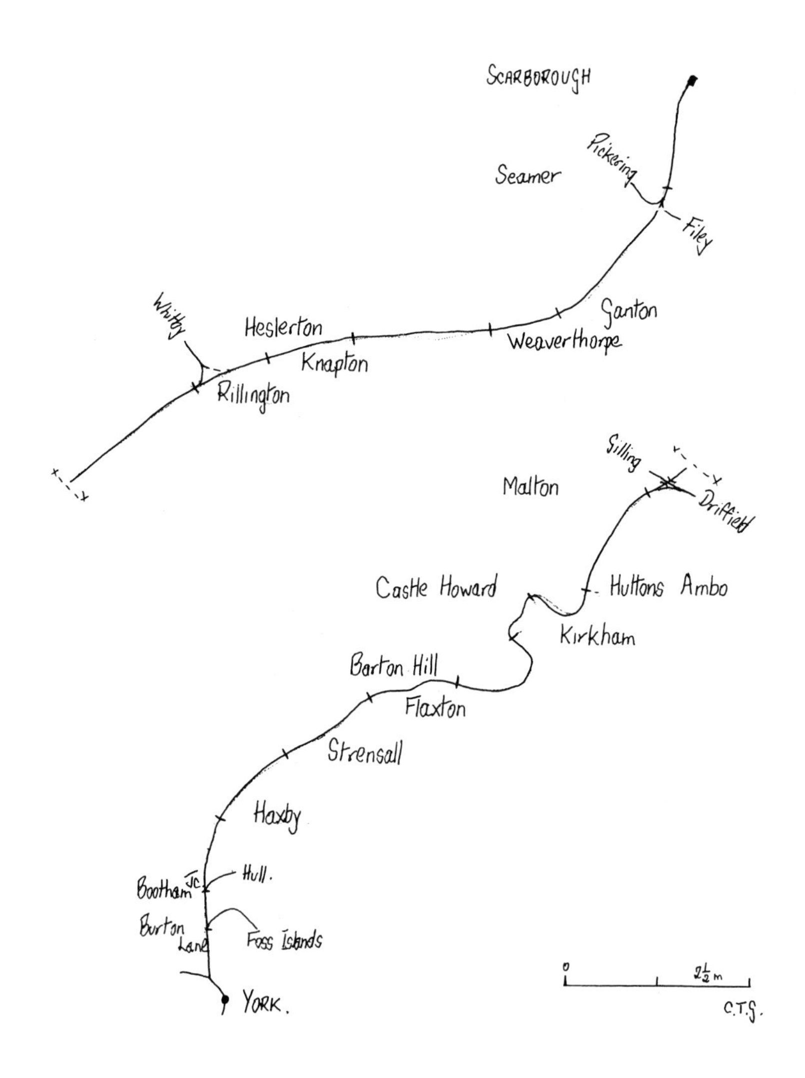
SCARBOROUGH
Pickering
Seamer
Filey
Whitby
Heslerton
Ganton
Knapton
Weaverthorpe
Rillington
Silling
Malton
Driffield
Castle Howard
Huttons Ambo
Kirkham
Barton Hill
Flaxton
Strensall
Haxby
Bootham Jc.
Hull.
Burton Lane
Foss Islands
YORK.
0
2½ m
C.T.G.

Contents.

Abbreviations.

GCR	Great Central Railway.
GNR	Great Northern Railway.
GNER	Great North of England Railway.
MR	Midland Railway.
NER	North Eastern Railway.
H&BR	Hull and Barnsley Railway.
LNER	London and North Eastern Railway.
YNMR	York and North Midland Railway.

The York and Scarborough Railway.

Scarborough is one of those places of which one never tires during repeated visits, and there is always something fresh to see and enjoy. The best memory of the town is perhaps the view from the seaward end of St.Nicholas street by the great Grand Hotel, where one can see the Castle, always appearing more than it really is, and the rich sweep of the South Bay with the two harbours below the entrance to North Marine Drive. The Castle is really the History of the town, its Keep and walls 80ft. high and 12ft. thick, being a major part. It was built by William le Gros in 1136, a baron who, in due course had his tenure seized by Henry II, who then built the Keep on its present site. In 1312, Edward II and his favourite, Piers Gaveston, landed at Scarborough in their flight from the barons. The latter gentleman took refuge in the fortress, was starved into submission and eventually lost his head. Later, in the Parliamentary Wars Sir Hugh Cholmley held the Castle for the King and was besieged by Sir John Meldrum who turned the nearby parish church into a battery for his own purposes. Sir John surrendered with honours in 1645, but in 1648 the new governor declared his allegiance to the King causing yet another battle to be fought, during which the Castle was taken and then dismantled. Later, George Fox, the first Quaker, was imprisoned there in 1665, suffering harsh treatment.

Glorious York in 1910. Petrol-electric motor-rail No. 3170 has arrived at platform 5 after working the 8.52 am Cawood - Selby - York arrival. Plenty of staff and notices on view. The Scarborough platforms are at the far end.

Photo: Nat. Railway Museum

Mossdale Hall, in the Castle yard and now in ruins, was the official residence, built in King John's reign. Its name comes from a governor of the Castle of 1397, when it was rebuilt. During the reign of the Young pretender in 1745 the Hall was rebuilt in brick as a barracks which long survived, manned by soldiers who in Victorian times, dispensed refreshment to thirsty tourists, as well as tall stories. Strangely, perhaps, the Castle was shelled by the Germans from the sea in 1914, adding to the ruins.

Later, the many tourists will be mentioned again, who came, and still do come flocking to the town, certainly not to see a mere Castle which is a wearisome 200ft. up for the very young and elderly. They would roll up for the sands and sea in both the North and South Bays, the former much better with, at one time a pleasure pier. The earlier, wealthier visitors would arrive in their own transport to visit the Spa, staying in one of the plushy hotels on the South Side near the source. The waters were in fact nothing to write home about: chalybeate and saline, beginning their popularity in a cistern in a small hut in 1698. Forty years on - the springs were lost beneath a landslip, then, refound they were in increasing use for a century until lost once more after a storm, whereafter the Cliff Bridge Company finally restored them and by 1858 Sir Joseph Paxton had appeared to set a Saloon and Promenade over the site. The former was destroyed by fire in 1876, to be replaced by the Pavilion in Turkish and Renaissance style with domes and detached tower, opened by the Lord Mayor of London in 1880. The complex contained a concert hall, restaurant and above, a small theatre and art gallery. The promenade when built was 200yd. long. After 1913 the Ballroom, for one thousand dancers, was constructed. From the gardens at this end of the town another fine view is obtainable.

Tourists will also seek out the parks at Peasholm and Northstead Manor where at various times there have been, and still are in some cases, sea battles with model ships, a tolerably realistic model railway, aerial lift for passengers and, sadly, the ruins of an open-air theatre. As the reader is obviously a railway enthusiast, the three cliff-lifts will be of interest, originally owned by the Scarborough Hydraulic Tramway Company and of great help to wheelchairs and buggies. The longest and most obvious one is at the side of the Grand Hotel, with a smaller one down the hill towards the Valley Bridge.

Early Days, Roads and Canals

In the early days Scarborough, like its partner Whitby to the north, would be quite self-contained with its own fishing fleet and locally generated industries, dependent on the sea and providing a secure refuge from winter storms. Unlike Whitby, however, Scarborough had a convenient means of communication inland to the south west through the immediate gap in the hills behind, then on to the Vale of Pickering and the lowlands of the river Derwent, a wayward stream which, though close to the sea, chose to flow the wrong way. The main road passed by this route, also the Pickering and Helmsley road which took the north side of the valley. Parliament took a hand in matters by passing the Turnpike Act of 1752 which included the care and upkeep of the Scarborough to York highway, while in 1702 an earlier Act had allowed interested parties to make the Derwent navigable for vessels of up to 50 tons between Barmby on the Ouse near Howden and Malton. The prime mover here was Thos. Wentworth and his successor, the 2nd. Earl Fitzwilliam, who lived some distance away near Barnsley, in South Yorkshire. and who owned the Silkstone colliery on the estate. The earl desired to bring the coal to Scarborough, hence the purchase of the canal rights. Malton was hardly the seaside town, so these rights were extended further to Yedingham Bridge in the centre of the plain, along a shallower stream which could, however, take 15 ton barges. The journey time for a barge of coal from Barnsley to Yedingham must have been lengthy, though once the output began to flow, provided it arrived regularly, then this would not matter, only perhaps to the bargee and his patient family en route. In 1840 Malton received some 38,000 tons, with cereals returning as ballast inland. The road was roughly as today, except that it cut across from Knapton through Yedingham to Snainton, where it picked up the road from Pickering to run directly into Scarborough. This was actually a sensible route, as the A64 before its final upgrading did include an awkward run north from Staxton up to Seamer village where there was a right turn. From 1840 a mail coach ran daily between York and Scarborough, with summer runs between the sea-side, Leeds and Sheffield. Fares were high, but as places on board were few, this mattered little. Once the primary route was in full swing, the others followed. That to Beverley being instituted from Seamer after a short time.

Whitby, being in a different situation as far as roads were concerned, was able to press for a railway with a good chance of success and with strong local backing. George Stephenson surveyed and built a line which began easily enough, then tackled the heights of Goathland with a rope-worked incline, moving on through Newtondale to reach Pickering, 24 miles in May 1836. Coaches would be waiting here to take passengers the further 26 miles to York. Fares for the through run were 13/- inside, 8/- outside, of which the railway could claim only 3/-.

B16 No. 61452 passes Kirkham Abbey

Railway Stirrings

In 1833 a proposal was made that a railway should be constructed to reach Scarborough from the Leeds & Selby Railway at Sherburn-in-Elmet, to run via Tadcaster, York and Malton. Nothing more was heard of this. Next, on 19th. 0ctober 1839 a public meeting was held in Scarborough Town Hall, at which George Stephenson and George Hudson (the famous) gave addresses. At this time the York & North Midland directors were financially committed to setting out the main line between Darlington and Newcastle, so that matters hung fire until 17th. November 1843, when a meeting decided to ask Parliament for powers to construct a line to Scarborough. Plans were soon prepared and were deposited in the right quarters by the end of the month.

The Y&NM had originated in York at a meeting with George Stephenson on 13th. October 1835, to settle the route of any line which would enable some link to be established with London and points south, be it eastwards via Lincoln and Cambridge, or westwards towards territory already being exploited, connecting with Rugby and the Midland Counties Railway. The latter option prevailed and it was agreed to lay a line as short as possible to run to the North Midland Railway main line from Sheffield to Leeds at Altofts near Normanton. Once this had been made clear, the field was then open for other schemes at York, and the new line was surveyed by Mr. Swanwick who had earlier carried out similar work on the Whitby & Pickering.

A named B1 passes Seamer Jc. with an excursion. The first coach is an ex GCR brake - third 'Barnun' coach of American style.

A8 No. 9864 hares off to Whitby from Rillington Jc.

The two major sponsors in the promotion of the York & Scarborough venture were James Meek, partner in York Glassworks, and George Hudson, twice Lord Mayor of York and local draper when not speculating, a hobby which he was well able to indulge in by virtue of an uncle's bequest. Both men quarrelled, Meek, a devout chapel man, objecting to Hudson's idea of running trains on Sundays, a practice which would have benefitted the artisans and labourers by providing a day out now and then, which in turn would have greatly cheered the Scarborough publicans and, cafe owners. Hudson himself profited, becoming sole Chairman and no doubt continuing to enhance his standing as a promoter over several years. His downfall came in 1849, a tragedy which fortunately did not affect many others.

George Stephenson and Hudson, after their public meeting in Scarborough, had to defer plans until the line from York to Newcastle had been commenced, the portion of what was the Great North of England Railway opening from York to Darlington, floated by Quaker money in 1841. Hudson himself subsidised the Newcastle & Darlington Junction Railway to push further north in 1844. As often happened at such times, there were dissenting voices against the railways, much as the outcries against new road schemes heard today. Mr. George Knowles knew his job; he was a civil engineer who had retired to the house 'Woodend' in Scarborough after designing and landscaping the South Cliff. As far as he could discern, the town had no wish for vagrants and those with no money to spend - no room here for the thought that 'the best things in life are free.'

Two schemes were on offer: the first, by John Rennie (son) of 29th. February 1840 was straightforward, but with a branch to Pickering. Both Stephenson and Hudson deposited plans as second idea, one via Pickering which added five miles to the through run, the second as anticipated but with a branch to Pickering. A tunnel of 1,100yd. would be driven beneath the village of Westow, to cross the Derwent nearby with a more southerly approach to York. Stephenson, who always liked a straight and level run, had his route crossing (as finally) at Low Hutton, but ironing out the bends with a tunnel of 1,430yd. below Whitwell Hill to regain what became the final route at Barton Hill.

On 17th. November 1843, with the final plan deposited, curves and all for the third time, Hudson decided to go ahead, greatly admired and as financially sound as he could appear to be. YNM shareholders weighed in with £260,000, the plans being passed by Parliament in the name of Robert Stephenson (for safety) without objection. To save money, all roads but three would be crossed on the level, while, to save the cost of tunneling, the line would curve along with the river, through the Howardian hills, the penalty being a permanent 40mph. speed limit.

Haxby Station with push and pull ready to leave

The first station at York was a small terminus set just inside the City wall with its entrance facing roughly south, so that YNM trains had easy access, whereas GNER trains from the north west curved round fairly easily to the platforms and their own coal depot. The York-Scarborough branch would come across the Ouse from the north and curve westwards into the GNE, since there was an engine shed and sundry depots in the way of its running due south to the parent YNM line. In either case York & Scarborough trains would be unable to run directly into the station, with the result that, once on the GNE they would have to reverse round into the terminus or come out in reverse as the case might be. The drawbacks of such a manoeuvre were soon evident; to begin with, it made such workings reliant on the good will of the GNE, day after day. Suggestions were already afoot that the York-Scarborough trains might come in over a more northerly sweep round by way of Clifton. The local landowner, Earl de Grey and residents were not impressed by this. Neater still would have been a straight junction with the GNE at Skelton which was even further north, but this was rejected by Parliarnent as making the new line too obviously dependent on a 'foreign' company. Within a short time all these petty difficulties would disappear like so many bubbles.

Strensall, with builder's notice announcing new developments

York - Scarborough Proposals

The bill for the York & Scarborougrh Railway was passed on 29th. March 1844 and opposed dutifully by Earl de Grey in the Lords. However, it was eventually approved and received the Royal Assent on 4th. July 1844. Further approval was given to a part of the route confirmed on 7th. July 1845 after four years of vagueness, namely the stretch along Bootham by the hospital grounds, one month before the line opened. The troubles, generated over whether to reverse or not at York were suddenly resolved when Hudson leased the GNE and brought the company into the fold. The Whitby & Pickering had also been sold to the YNM at a knock-down price during this time.

The line was to be built in four sections, presumably York to Barton Hill, Barton Hill to Malton, Malton to Seamer and Seamer to Scarborough. The tender was won by Joseph Crawshaw of Dewsbury, who offered a discount of 5% if awarded all four, at a total cost of £61,682. This gentleman had previously built stage one of the YNM main line from York to Copmanthorpe, so that ready evidence of the quality of his work was available. There were three road bridges and three river bridges for the 0use at York, the Derwent at Low Hutton and the station approach bridge at Malton. In 42 miles there were only bridges of minor size in total. Things were done quite cheaply at a total cost, including the Pickering branch, of only £2,382 per rnile. By October 1844 the whole course of the line had been plotted and all was cut and dried, apart from the temporary confusion at the York end, where Stephenson saved time by building a cast iron girder bridge over the river instead of elegant brick arches.

The Derwent canal came into its own at Malton, where at its head near the station baulks of fir were brought up from Hull to construct the river bridges. Here in Malton lived the resident Engineer, Alfred Dickens, younger brother of the famous novelist. Around Malton there was a wooden structure at the station approach, a low viaduct at Norton east of the station and the more important bridge at Low Hutton to the south west, which was to be of cast iron but cheapened by Hudson to wood in August 1844. The Norton bridge was ready in December. Overall supervision of design lay in the hands of John Birkinshaw, Robert Stephenson's assistant, who was based in York.

There were no real problems until the last lap at Seamer, where rnarshy land was met towards Scarborough. The Mere was anywhere and everywhere, ill defined and calling for landscaping which came with a railway boundary on its west side, with much peat being removed in the process. Mr. P. Sharrock was in charge of the tasks at this end. At York, to allow for the piles of the Ouse bridge to be sunk, the river level had to be lowered for a time at Naburn, lower downstream. At first there was also a low brick viaduct of twelve arches constructed adjacent, which was gradually filled in over the years. So haste seems to have been in evidence during the building of the line, in fact the whole feature was completed in less than a year, though several matters were not really correct at the opening. A trial run was held on 12th. June 1845 from Bootham to Scarborough, with the official inspection by Major Gen. Pasley on 4th. July, at which everything appeared to pass muster, wooden bridges and all; even the Pickering branch was passed for horse drawn vehicles, which was evidently in order as they were still operating on the hilly section to Whitby. The Ouse bridge was thrown up in 14 weeks, as compared with the nearby road bridge at Micklegate which required as many years!

Of the original £260,000 set aside for the cost of the line, laid single at first, there was a surplus which, it was agreed could be put towards the cost of a branch to Bridlington; however, the terrain to be covered on this stretch would prove to be a different nut to crack.

Flaxton station

The Opening Run

After previous heavy rain, the opening day dawned clear and the whole city was on its feet as the Beckwith Peal rang loudly from York Minster. A good breakfast party had been arranged for 9 am. in the Guild Hall, with five long tables and a cross table at the head, at which sat George Hudson, Chairman, Sir John Lowther, Sir J.V.S. Johnstone, Sir F. Trench, H.R. Yorke (all of these MPs) and a 'vast number' of ladies and gentlemen. The original words, as reported in 'The Yorkshire Gazette' of the day, are worth quoting:

'After the breakfast was concluded arrangements were made for proceeding to the station. The ladies took their carriages and the gentlemen formed in order for a public procession from the Guildhall to the Railway Station, preceded by a band of music.'

The train, comprising 35 carriages, was in readiness at the appointed hour, and two powerful engines, 'The Hudson' and 'The Lion' had their steam up. The party was soon all comfortably seated and every preparatory arrangement for 'the start' having been made,at half past ten o' clock the huge, snake like body was seen making way with an imperceptibly accelerated speed, and stealing along under the broad, Tudor arch which carries the city ramparts over the railway. Crowds of people thronged the walls, and every position from which a view of the train could be had.

A fine turnout for the camera at Barton Hill. The original signal box and level crossing with an interesting little signal box.

Some little delay was occasioned, necessarily, to getting the train on to the Scarborough line from the Great North of England Railway - the junction being, in our opinion extremely inconvenient and one which it will soon be found requisite to alter. It is due, however, to the directors that this is not the junction which they proposed to parliament, but one which was forced upon them by the opposition of the GNER. The train having been brought safely on to the new line it speedily reached the bridge across the Ouse. Thousands of persons were here collected to witness the passage across the river by so heavy a train. The sight was most imposing; and the line through Bootham and for some distance in the vicinity of York was lined by persons who had taken up their position, according to their taste, to witness the passing train. At all the village stations there was also a grand 'turn out' to witness the opening train, *and no little amazement was displayed by many at the novelty and grandeur of the scene. After running about an hour the train reached the Castle Howard station, where the signal 'to stop' was given, and the hospitality of the Earl of Carlisle was evinced by a profuse supply of strong ale from the cellars of Castle Howard for all who chose to partake. Lord Morpeth with a large party here took their seats in the train, and after a short detention it was again in motion. On nearing the town of Malton there were further manifestations of rejoicing. From the steeple of St. Leonards Church there were several flags suspended; the bells rang a merry peal; a band of music was at the station and the folks of Malton were mustered in great numbers to welcome the party from York. A number of gentlemen who had been invited to join in the opening trip, here entered the carriages, and after the tenders had taken in a supply of water the train was again in motion.*

At Rillington a triumphal arch was erected, at Sherburn there was a band of music, a handsome display of banners and a very large assembly of people. At Ganton there was displayed a large banner inscribed 'Long live the Queen', and a band of music was stationed in an orchestra erected for the occasion.(sic) Here again, the train stopped and took up Sir Thomas Legard and party from Ganton Hall. Passing Seamer, the railway became thronged with parties who had come from Scarborough to meet the train, and as it traversed the valley, crowds of people lined the higher ground - Oliver's Mount was a favourite resort for the more active, and from its elevation no doubt the train would be distinguished for many miles. Entering the cutting beyond Washbeck viaduct the

D 49 No. 62762 passes Kirkham Abbey

assembly became more dense and the banks were literally crowded. A large detachment of York police, under the direction of Mr. Chalk, Chief Constable, was in attendance; a number of special constables connected with the borough of Scarborough were also on duty, and the utmost order and regularity were maintained.'

In Scarborough the day was marked as a public holiday with all shops closed, the streets thronging with townsfolk and visitors, some of whom had travelled in by sea. At noon the Mayor led a procession to the station to await the arrival of the train, boosting the crowd to around 15,000. George Hudson and his directors were taken on arrival to a reception room at the station, where the Mayor gave formal thanks for the benefits which the railway was to bestow on his township, to which Hudson replied that his aim was always to meet the wishes of the people, in this case folk who had been most courteous and helpful in so many ways. Subsequently the party proceeded to one end of the station which had been roofed over specially for the occasion, and where tables had been carefully set up and laid by Mrs. Reed the caterer. Here, at the luncheon, the top table included Lord Morpeth and the Lord Mayor of York. Hudson, in his concluding speech, said that the event was a significant one in the history of Scarborough which would be greatly to the advantage of its inhabitants, as well as to the people of York and the West Riding, enabling them readily to enjoy 'the healthy breezes of the sea'.

A complete view of Castle Howard.

Meanwhile, the unmentioned train crews and guards would be trying to fathom a means of running round 35 coaches, four wheelers roughly the length of a dozen modern vehicles, in readiness for the return journey. Quite likely the engines would have returned tender first. The same newspaper from which the above quote came, gave the list of stations with the arrival time at each:

	Miles from York	Arrival Time
Clifton	1	10.48 am
Haxby	5	11.00
Strensall	7	11.12
Flaxton	10	11.25
Barton	12	11.34
Howsham	14	11.40
Kirkham	15	11.46
Castle Howard	16	11.50
Hutton	19	12.10 pm
Malton	21	12.17
Rillington	26	12.45
Knapton	28	12.50
Heslerton	30	12.55
Sherburn	33	1.00
Ganton	35	1.07
Seamer	39	1.22
Scarborough	42	1.35

Frills and furbelows at Cranbeck Gatehouse

'There was no attempt at great speed. Under the direction of Mr. Cabry, resident engineer of the YNMR and Mr. Birkinshaw', engineer of the Scarborough line, the train was taken throughout the distance with the greatest comfort to the passenger and without the slightest casualty occurring.'

Note the station at Howsham, at the gates and possibly opened specially to please George Hudson who was born at Scrayingham nearby. The halt disappeared after 1849. Clifton is another early entrant which soon vanished.

The original station at Scarborough was built after Hudson's early period at York, of two platforms with two centre storage sidings linked at each end in the fashion of the time by small turntables on to which vehicles might be moved manually from line to line. The admin. building ran along where it exists at the present time. There were two hipped roofs and a back wall with a loading platform. Malton, the principal country station, had a 40 ft. all-over roof and two tracks served by a platform each side with water towers for engine refreshment at each end. The admin. building was single storey, as surviving at present with a two

Huttons Ambo Station. The river bridge is just visible on the right.

storey building at one end for the station master. The line was initially single, with three trains each way and one on Sundays and with excursion traffic almost from the outset; on 5th August the first special came down from Newcastle, harbinger of many more from the north country. George Hudson may have been grasping financially, but his altruism was genuine enough and he gave the people of York the Royal Agricultural Show in 1848, providing a special station for the purpose at Bootham (Clifton?) where in fact foundations had been put in place for a permanent structure on a nearby overbridge, though further progress was hampered by local protests in 1846.

Further haste to complete, as well as in the single track, was evident in the bridges: as noted, the Ouse structure was rushed into position, while that at Low Hutton was built as a three span low structure of wood in September 1844. One of the abutments collapsed, so that a fourth span had to be added to bring the site of the offending support further back from the edge. Nearer Malton the Derwent had an ox-bow loop cut by two low viaducts, again of wood, and a new straight cut for the canal was introduced here. This bridging later disappeared beneath an embankment infill. In 1867 the Low Hutton bridge was replaced by wrought iron girders, and latterly by plate. Likewise, the wooden bridge linking

Malton station with the town became a wrought iron one in 1870. Before ridding itself of the river, as it were, the railway straightened out the rather meandering and muddy course followed east of the station through Norton, keeping it to the north side and, in 1868, raising the track somewhat to avoid flooding here.

Malton gained in importance in the 1850s when the Malton & Driffield Jc. Railway opened, promoted by local landowners under the Chairmanship of Lord Morpeth of Castle Howard. Engineering on the line, which was heavy in places, was carried out by Birkinshaw and Dickens, though the former left eventually, leaving Dickens the literal spadework, including the mile long tunnel at Burdale. The line was largely an almost complete waste of effort, in spite of Hudson's promise of £40,000 from the YNM which would almost certainly have been forthcoming to make the project a working reality The line opened on 19th May 1853 simultaneously with the Thirsk-Malton branch from the GNE at Pilmoor which was completed a year or two after Hudson's decline and resultant financial upheaval. The two branches met end-on over the Derwent in Norton, and the Ryedale line especially could be used as a route for holiday trains avoiding York by reversing at Malton on to the Scarborough line.

Quite a busy Malton station with the crossing bridge in position.

In 1854 a two road shed was built at Malton for four engines, while the odd two storey building at the front end of the station was matched by a new one at the other housing a refreshment room and staff quarters.

Trains from Whitby ran on to Malton in 1862 instead of to Rillington; at this time the station was rebuilt, with the main station platform built out over the site of the Scarborough line up to the old York line which now changed its use and direction. On the other side of this was built an island, giving the new Scarborough line two faces and an outer face for a new Up line to York out in the open. It is obvious that the island platform was built to disguise the supporting pillars of the all-over roof, though it did produce an unusual station plan. At the east end of the station was an inset Driffield/Whitby bay with two adjacent carriage sidings, all covered over. The Driffield service, operated by the 'Malton Dodger', was infrequent, as indeed were the runs off the line from Pilmoor and Gilling. These would reverse at Scarborough Road Jc. and come down a spur to Malton East. Soon the spur was lengthened towards the level crossing, and by using a crossover on the spur here it was possible to carry out operations with the pilot engine without closing the gates unduly.

The Malton Gas Company moved its coal supply from canal to rail in 1866, using in turn the Brancepeth colliery in the north, then Fitzwilliam's Silkstone colliery at prices one third cheaper than the water transport. As with almost all canals at this time, the railway proved itself superior in every way, causing a reduction in the price of coal cartage, from 1/8- to 1/4- per ton, but still managing a loss of two thirds of income in 1846. Six years later, 17,000 tons of coal reached Malton by canal, but the operation was unprofitable. It was left to the NER to buy out the canal for £40,000 and effectively stifle any competition. Scarborough had had similar problems, though much later, in 1873 when the town's gas works had moved from the harbour where it had been fed by coal brought by coasters, to the station area, and even then some coastwise coal had continued to reach the town by 1900, up to 1,700 tons.

Early Stations at Scarborough & York

While visiting Scarborough, so to speak, it is opportune to review the developments here over the years, which are many and piecemeal. As already noted, the first station was a basic, two platform affair with two sidings which had to cope with a great amount of seasonal traffic for the first 14 years up to 1859, when the long No.1 excursion platform was opened, together with a large open concourse fronting Westborough. Next, No. 2 platform was added alongside, the line flanked on both sides to allow easy access and alighting. No. 3 was the original, old arrival platform, while the old departure platform was removed and it became a carriage siding, since storage space was vital. It all sounds small, but remember that No. 1 and 2 would be much longer.

Block working was introduced in 1873, with trains signalled by bell code from box to box, and in 1878 Scarborough station was resignalled in that lavish NER fashion with plenty of miniature arms and imposing gantries. A new roof went over platforms 2 and 3 in August 1879. After this came a new engine shed and an extra running line into the station. A new roof also covered No.1 platform, with an official access from Westborough. All new ironwork was supplied by Handyside of Derby.

Little Houlbeckfield carries its hefty nameboard

The Architect was William Bell, who performed an ingenious task quite well in blending his own ideas with the style of G.T. Andrews. A matching veranda was added to the 1859 train shed, while off came a glass awning at the front of the building and sent off to Malton; instead came along three pavilions in the Andrews style, the end one housing the toilets, gents. at the north side, the centre being the entrance marked by a tall bulbous clocktower rising amaryllis-like and called by one of the Sitwells of 'Woodend' Luxembourg Classic style. This flower blossomed in 1883. Not inappropriately, perhaps, the station master at this time of change was Mr Bearup. Early in 1881 a new engine shed was built adjacent to Seamer road south of the station, a half roundhouse of thirteen roads (i.e. not 26) round a 44 ft. 8 in. turntable. Next, in 1888 a straight shed was ordered to house a further 24 engines near the site of the other, while outside was placed a 50 ft. turntable, which was in turn replaced in 1924 by a 60 ft. version meant for Goole, though as it is not certain as to where it would be likely to fit in the layout at that port, it was probably a wrong order. Any large engines which appeared would be dealt with by using outriggers, though a 'Pacific No. 2795, 'Call Boy' caused embarrassment in the summer of 1934 by arriving unannounced from Glasgow via Malton, was unable to turn and had to return to York tender first with the rolling stock. Latterly, a 70 ft. turntable was installed for steam specials.

At the end of the last century platforms 4 and 5 were added to the layout where the former carriage sidings had been, these being used for the Whitby trains which had begun to run on the route opened along the coast on 16th July 1885, through a tunnel to Falsgrave signal box, where they reversed and backed in across the layout. The Scarborough & Whitby Company was a private one and had already earmarked a site north of the tunnel at Gallows Close for an independent terminus and goods depot. The NER, fuelled by the spirit of Hudson's early enterprise, bought out this land to use for its own depot, which it opened in June 1899 with a new and spacious shed having bays in it 234 ft. long.The older goods shed at the station was thus made redundant, so that the end wall could now be opened out to house two further platforms, Nos. 8 and 9, with Nos. 6 and 7 between the two adjacent buildinge filled in under a linking roof. Along Seamer roadside various sets of carriage sidings had appeared on the Up and three on the Down side of the line, with a slightly later set of nine Down for the season of 1898. These were all near the gas works which was at last linked to rail at about this time.

Rillington manages to look very much abandoned

Traffic in Edwardian times became so brisk with duplicates called into service at short notice by York and Hull, that a new station was required at Scarborough, for which the NER happened to have purchased land on the south side at Westwood, approximately where Tesco stands today. Unfortunately, since the earlier acquisition villas had been built further along, preventing good rail access, with the result that the company had, once more, to build on the north side adjacent to Westborough, but this time further out beyond the tunnel, so that trains would in fact now be able to halt, unload and run on empty into new carriage sidings beyond the tunnel at Gallows Close. Here were ten new sidings and a 60 ft. turntable. The station, known as Londesborough Road but also as Washbeck (see p.) opened 8th June 1908 with one long through platform and bay beneath a lightly constructed roof, all at a cost of £7,634. It was, however, noticeable at times that passengers were confused as to which station to report to for their returning train, this aggravated by the lack of a direct pedestrian link between the two, and even when the names were clearly marked on the tickets problems could arise. Eventually the station was used for block arrivals such as works parties, where a supervisor was in charge on board.

A whole book could be written about York station, once the largest in the world and possessing to this day a wonderful atmosphere caused by noise, light and shadowplay beneath the impressive steel arches which nobody up to now has seen fit to tamper with, except Hitler, at one end of the vastness. From being a Roman burial ground the site had come a long way, though a wag might consider that the present National Railway Museum which enjoys part of it with its collection of fossilised rolling stock is keeping the use of the site correctly, as desired in the best towns and cities.

Back now to the original terminal station, which soon saw improvements after George Hudson had leased the GNE in 1845. The YNM coal depot could now be closed and a second arch made in the wall alongside the first, so that the station might be enlarged to a total of five platforms with bays for the Scarborough trains. Lines to a new goods depot passed through the new arch. Outside, the YNM and GNE were linked by a new line curving from one to the other, but Scarborough trains still had to reverse in and out. In 1866 an Act was obtained to replace the station by a through one, a radical move which was, however delayed by lack of funds because of investment in developments around Leeds. The Act was revived in 1871 and the new station opened on 25th June 1877, a whole new complex for passengers, goods, coal and engine servicing. How popular the Scarborough trains must have been, carrying the reversals through the construction site, and how happy the travellers to see the upheaval en route to and from work!

The Ouse bridge was rebuilt and Thief Lane straightened out, becoming Leeman Road in the process, named after the Chairman of the NER, and Marble Arch where it passed beneath the junction of rails at the north end. The track had been raised by four feet generally. The first train out of the new York station was to Scarborough, the 5.30 am., with many folk booking tickets to Haxby to be the first passengers out.

Knapton station with the grain silos

Along the line: York - Castle Howard.

Time now to traverse the line once more, this time more leisurely than as described on the Opening Day. It always seems odd that the LNER chose to close a block of stations in 1930, on a line which passed at one end through a developing area, though admittedly the potential was feeble east of Malton. The prettier parts where the line curved could have enticed ramblers, but no doubt the company considered that the nuisance value of stopping trains at busy times was perhaps too great to tolerate. It was a pity, however, that other lines in the area such as the Malton-Driffield and the Pilmoor-Malton with even less potential were able to soldier on for a further twenty years or so. The stations to Scarborough did in fact retain their platforms and goods facilities, as did others closed at the same time, such as those on the H & B, and were available for excursions, with tickets printed and issued by the retained staff.

The Scarborough line set off from two portions of the layout at York; the end-on junction with the goods lines and running lines from the western platforms which crossed acutely the East Coast main line, and the ends of the set of three bay platforms at the north end, east side, both under the eye of Waterworks signal box, built originally in the rather fancy style of an extended octagonal shape with ornamental barge boards. The cabin was demolished in 1938 in connection with the projected station alterations which never came because of wartime, leaving a temporary affair which lasted until 1951. There was also another signal box nearby, Leeman Road, which most likely handled the Down side traffic only. Waterworks' Down Scarborough home signal, just beyond the cabin, appears from photographs to have been renewed and raised significantly in height over the years.

Once out of York the line crosses the Ouse and enters a cutting with retaining wall and railings, keeping company with the two hospitals on the right. Burton Lane Jc. (1705 yd. from Waterworks) was at one time a level crossing before becoming junction for the Foss Islands branch of 8th December 1879 which went off sharply right round to the south east, then south, serving firstly Rowntree's Cocoa Works, cattle market, sand siding, gas works and the railway laundry, before running to the Layerthorpe station of the Derwent Valley Light Railway, which dated from 1913. All the other concerns evolved at different times, Rowntree's had a works halt just round the corner on the branch, which dealt with workfolk each day from 1927. The level crossing at Burton Lane was replaced by an overbridge to a new housing estate in 1930, when the signal box was moved south to the actual junction with the branch line. This was double for the first few yards with a short loop off left to take in the works platform and ground frame. York City football ground is away to the left. Distances given are from signal box to signal box. Further on was Bootham Junction (919 yd.) at Wigginton Road level crossing set on a skew, heralded by the main crossover which was isolated from the junction points beyond with the cabin on the right and the double line off, the route to Market Weighton of 11th October 1847. This route to Hull only reached Beverley 28 years later, after heavy engineering across the Wolds, in 1865. The Market Weighton route was closed exactly a century after opening to great disappointment as its revenue and future potential were both promising. At Bootham was the site of the early station of 1848 serving the Stray.

Running north and Haxby Gates was met, at the south end of a straggling and large village (the cabin was called Haxby Road, while along the road to the south is the suburb-cum-village of New Earswick

An old view of Heslerton station with some passengers

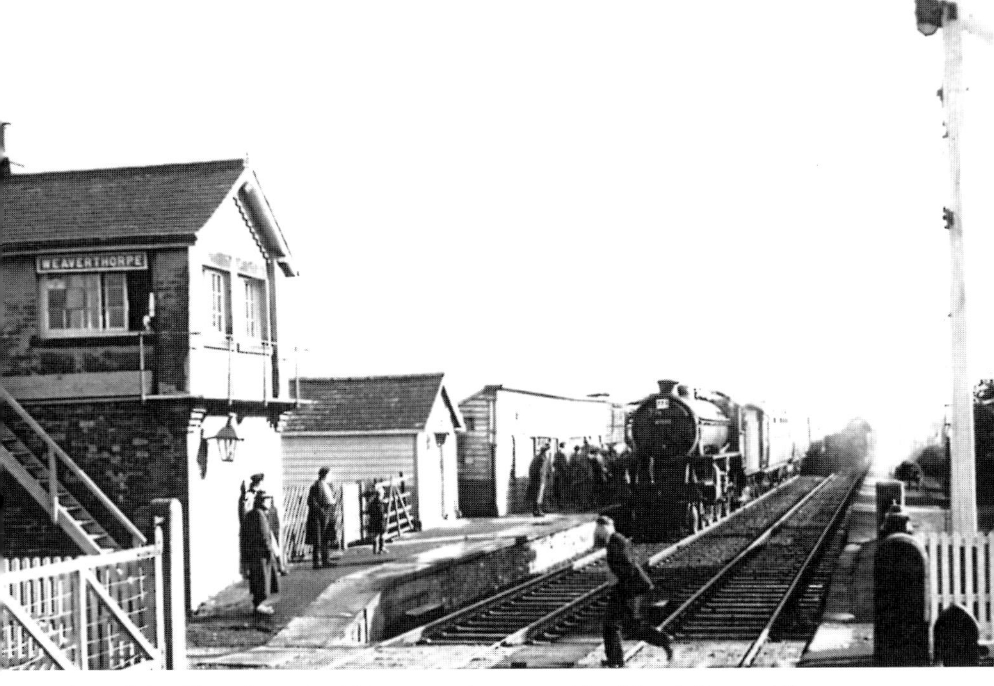

A special at Weverthorpe is picking up on the wrong side of the platform, while a mysterious collection of rolling stock appears to be about to pass.

which had its own station on the Hull line. Haxby station (2 m. 1036 yd.) was at the far end of its village, very convenient. The station building and coal drops were at the west side of the line, with platforms staggered so that stopping trains could run beyond the level crossing to clear it. Originally there was a flagged area in front of the station building for the times when passengers did not mind climbing up and dropping off! In 1912 a proposal was made for a light railway to Brandsby (see p. 54).

Between Haxby and Strensall the Foss, which has been meandering nearby, is crossed by a low bridge, after which it virtually vanishes further along. Then follow two level crossings, the second of which had a small signal box, Strensall No. 2 (1 m.1610 yd.) on the outskirts of Strensall village, where was situated Strensall Halt, the bare minimum of standing area, though even this managed to be staggered so that the railbus might draw past in 1926, and for a few years afterwards. The reason for the halt would probably have been to serve the large army camp to the south on the common, not big enough for a brigade to stand on, but more likely for the use of civilian workers commuting to and from York. The larger troop movements would be dealt with at Strensall station (882 yd.) a short way further on, where the far end of the large village, similar in size to Haxby, was coming to an end. Wartime brought much military traffic to Strensall, with 150,000 in 1915, continuing traffic after closure, including 5,000 in 1935 and many more in the 1939-45 conflict. The station had a refuge siding on the west side, followed by the station house, crossing, Scarborough platform and largish yard with coal drops, headshunt and run-round and the Littlethorpe brickworks of 1901, for which the layout was adapted at the time. On the east side was the York platform, crossing, signal box rebuilt in 1902 and long refuge siding.

Strensall really marks the end of suburban York, though local services did in fact reverse at Flaxton, the next station, in order to keep out of the way for a time. The line turns north east across the top edge of Strensall common, over Common Lane and Flaxton Moor crossings to reach Flaxton (2 m. 892 yd.), a linear village along one side of the road to the south with common land and cattle grids at each end of it. Such stations would generate traffic by gig and wagonette from distant villages, and farm produce such as sugar and potatoes. At Flaxton the platforms were parallel, met first before the crossing and followed by a potato dock and the first goods shed in the yard on the left, the signal box and relief siding on the right. The station house was on the north side of the line, away from the village which was a good half mile away. For a time the 10.40 am. from Scarborough stopped conditionally at Flaxton to allow the NER magistrate to attend the Bulmer East Petty sessions, then held at the village.

Ganton station looking east

The curious assembly of buildings at Seamer.

Beyond Flaxton are crossings at Thornton and Foston Gates, before the line turns due east preparatory to its series of curves, at the original crossing with the Scarborough road, today's A64 at Barton Hill (2m. 614 yd.), an interesting spot, actually isolated from the village of Barton-le-Willows to the south by a whole mile. The first layout was orthodox enough, with a long refuge siding on the south side, then a crossing with signal box on the north side with parallel platforms and station house of basic terrace appearance on the Scarborough platform with the station nameboard blazoned across it at first floor level. Beyond was a small yard on the north side with a dock and coal drops; a curiosity here was the lane down to the village which crossed the middle of the yard and the running lines, presumably all hand-worked. Here was in fact the first Barton station which can only have lasted for a few early years. Come 1936 and the North Riding County Council began to carry out big road improvements to the trunk road, placing a sweeping overbridge across the site of the station and yard, causing the old signal box to close on 10th November 1936. This led to some reduction of pointwork in the yard (see plan) and a new signal box of up-to-date LNER style with metal windows to replace the old one by the Barton lane at the south side beyond the gates, thus a third of a mile east of the original cabin. The yard gates here were still hand worked and the signalman had to emerge for this infrequent duty, though working the running line gates by the usual wheel. In 1965 when the yard had gone, early lifting barriers were installed here. Even today the signal box has a 'just installed' modern air about it.

Crossing next at Plain Moor and Howsham as the line turns through south east round to north east by Howsham village. Only in 1996 was it still possible, on a line busy with 158 units to ring the bell at Howsham Gates for attention and have the lady emerge from her cabin, pure NER, to open each gate in turn, furthest one first. George Hudson was born at Scrayingham, but it would have been quicker to sail up the Derwent to Howsham from there rather than attempt the winding trip by road. Howsham Hall, a very fine building, is visible in its park on the right as we curve round to the north, then north west into a narrowing valley with the river on the right to reach Kirkham Abbey, perhaps the most beautiful spot on the line, with a good vista of both river and railway from the Abbey area. As the station house is now a garden centre, no great excuse is needed to pay a visit here. The small settlement of Kirkham is near the abbey ruins, while on the other side of the line - even here the NER managed a level crossing - lies Whitwell-on-the-Hill beyond the fast and noisy A64 at the end of a steep climb. The Derwent used to have a lock here for river traffic; now it is a weir. The station catered for day trippers in earlier times who would come to admire the ruins (admission optional in 1900), or ramble by the water. Perhaps, too they might have hired a boat from the signalmen here, who had bought on the cheap one of the lifeboats from the old 'Mauretania' for such purposes, or they could seek out the station master for fishing tackle or simply buy stamps and postcards to send home. It might even be correct to surmise that the station master's wife supplied tasty cream teas! It was certainly a change from hiring out sacks to farmers or manipulating the stocks of coal for villagers. First of all came the York side platform, then the crossing followed by the signal box left (3 m. 692 yd.) and the station house of lime stone on the right, basically an end-on terrace structure with a bay window on the end overlooking the activities and a single storey side entrance from the road. The Scarborough platform was opposite, complete with open-fronted waiting shed, adjacent to the signal box of 1873 and still working, while beyond on the right was a small yard with end loading dock and coal drops.

On leaving here the train would completely change its direction on a long right hand curve with a 40 mph. limit. The next station was Castle Howard, not a village but built to serve the stately home some three miles away along private roads. The station was minimal in layout, with, first a single siding and loading dock, the station building left and parallel platforms. The signal box (1338 yd) closed 12th September 1960. It was opposite the station house which was a 'one off' in the Italianate style, with an opera singer's gallery billowing out at first floor level over the platform edge and, above it, a small campanile.

The side entrance was a porch with a room above it, while parallel to the platform on the other side was a single storey extension with the usual offices. The building obviously sought to impress but managed also to look insipid in its limestone and rather heavyhandedness. The coal drops were further on, at Crambeck (732yd.), signal box on the left and coal drops opposite by the river. The box closed on 28th. February 1971. Deliveries had been brought here by barge long before the railway, for the Earl of Carlisle at the big house. The Crambe beck comes down here to join the river, while nearby is a pretty gatekeeper's house with ornimental barge boards. Round the bend now, south east and at the side of the hill was the sand siding of the Castle Howard Sond Co., worked by ground frame (961 yd.). The Burythorpe Sand Co., had plans for a light railway in the area, which died at the onset of the Great War (see p. 55).

The tower and roofline at Scarborough.

Malton & Rillington

The railway can now get into its stride as it leaves the closeness of the valley and heads towards Malton, reaching Huttons Ambo which served High and Low Hutton on the left side of the line and a short distance away; Low was nearer, High is up by the main road. The river is crossed by the bridge as speeds increase to 75 mph. Menethorpe village is on the other side of the water, and to discourage villagers from using the railway as a short cut across the river, the NER built a footbridge to accommodate them. Hutton station was rudimentary with a side dock to a refuge siding on the left opposite the signal box on the right (1m. 1063 yd.). Then follows a road underbridge and station with parallel platforms, the single storey builing of two gables on the west side, rather low down due to the platform in front having been raised over the years. The station house behind was of the normal pattern. En route to Malton the line cut off an oxbow of the Derwent, thus isolating three railwaymen's houses which were left with no means of access other than by rail.

Malton has always been a busy place on a crossroads to Whitby, York, Scarborough, Helmsley and Driffield. It has Roman origins in the old settlement of Derwentio and what is regarded as New Malton is 800 years old, rebuilt after troubles with the Scots. The town lies on the river and railway, which is in fact in Norton, East Yorkshire, here a town every bit as large as its close neighbour. For a time Malton was in the top five stations on the NER for handling livestock, with 124,000 being processed in 1914; this traffic is reflected in the cattle and horse docks provided in the extensive goods yard. The railway afforded employment at one time to over 100 in the town. Today there are just three.

First signal box met with was Malton West (2m. 841yd.) which dealt with the turn-in and exit to the goods yard at the north side of the layout, curving round to buffers by the river's edge. West box also routed trains from the Up independent running line from East on the other side, on to the main line. The engine shed and turntable, as well as outlets from three private sidings, horse dock and coal drops were all to the south of the station. Down trains ran through the train shed flanked by platform faces which were linked across by a barrow way interlocked to the signalling when in use, saving a walk for passengers and staff alike. The

Up main had an outer platform face on the island, which had a short bay at the York end. There was also a Whitby and Driffield bay under roofing at the east end, where a small yard with goods shed was situated. The latter lines came in at Malton East. In the centre of the station layout was a third cabin, Malton Station (553 yd.) which seems to have had the least work of the three.

Malton East (473yd.) had its level crossing, then the double track junction to the Driffield line off right rising parallel to the main line to reach Scarborough Road cabin (904yd.) The difficulties at East can be imagined on a summer Saturday. A solid stream of road traffic both ways with gate movements for excursions being brought down from the Ryedale line with a pilot engine on the rear, over the crossing and reverse right away, with possibly other trains waiting for passage. Times changed, however; the goods shed in the bigger yard was burnt down in 1956, while the engine shed closed in 1963, the last steam working to Whitby being a return trip with No. 43055. The branch closed in 1965, the Driffield line having succumbed years before. Malton's Big Day came in 1978 when the new by-pass was opened, easing the strain through Norton. The larger goods yard in front of the station had three cattle roads, three coal drops and seven lines round the goods shed for general traffic. Today Malton is basic, with a regular service, all trains using the one platform adjacent to the listed building, though the all-over roof has gone.

Auto No. 67332 on Driffield outs train in the bay at Malton August 1949
Photo: M. Black

D49 No. 62770 passes Huttons Ambo on a Scarborough train
Photo: J.W. Armstrong

Once they have shaken the rust and dust of Malton off their wheels, trains can now extend themselves on the fairly straight, level and uninteresting section of line as far as the curve before Seamer, running at up to 90mph. in a north easterly direction. The aspect is reminiscent of the flat stretch east of Redhill, through the Kentish countryside, without the hops. Under the Ryedale line bridge, single track girders with double line abutments, under the later by-pass and off along the four miles to Rillington Jc., broken up in its time by ' block splitters', the small cabin of Houlbeckfield (1m. 949yd.) south of the line and a later one, Espersykes which was north of the line and only opened in high season, disappearing in 1928. The former cabin was in time reduced to summer working and eventually closed. The company must have been desperate at times to come up with a good name for a signal box, since Houlbeckfield does not appear as a label on maps, though Espersykes is a farm a good mile or two away on the other side of the river.

Rillington has six level crossings in almost two miles, which is probably a record. The village is largish, situated a short way away to the south east on the A64 and would not have guaranteed much rail traffic. The station is a puzzle in several ways, firstly at the junction point of the

Whitby line which ran off north at the east end, with its signal box (2m. 1164yd.) on the south side, dock and bay platform opposite and Down siding which ran back into the Up branch to give an optional reversing place. Near the signal box was a coal drop and Up siding. To the west of the station site on the south side was a goods shed with two sidings. West of the station one of the perky little NER wooden cabins worked the station level crossing. With parallel platforms and nearby junction it must have struck someone that the place should have an overall roof, decidedly odd in the circumstances, but no doubt with passengers in mind who wished to change trains and, possibly, any future developments. Needless to say, the Whitby bay had no form of roof. The station house was at the side of the road, built to support its end of the roof with two bay windows side by side for surveying the platform. It may have been that someone in the engineering department had a set of roof parts to dispose of; one thing is certain, the place had atmosphere and it would have been a joy to hear B16s roar through on summer Saturdays. It was soon decided that passengers should change at Malton, and a new curve was also built from the Scarborough line to the east, round to join the Whitby line northwards, thus avoiding any needless changing. The curve was opened in July 1865, but faced with a daily average of only 31 passengers, the service stopped a year later, the trackwork going in 1880, just before the Forge Valley line was opened from Seamer to give easier access to Pickering. Woolly thinking seems to have been in play at this time, nor did it clear much later on when in 1959 a brand new signl box was built and opened at Rillington, west of the station to replace the two earlier cabins, large and small, at each end. Staff here were housed in a smart terrace of houses, a memorial to a fascinating place still visible on the north side of the line.

D17 No. 1921 at rest in a NE roundhouse

Over the Straight

Beyond Rillington came Scampston High and Low Gates, past the site of Scampston Jc. where the spur left, round to Marishes Jc.

Knapton West and East and Scampston, small villages were a short way off to the south of the line served by Knapton station (1m. 1598 yd.) at the level crossing of the old road to Yedingham, where the Derwent canal ended. First met was a small yard on the south side, then signal box north of the line, the level crossing and parallel platforms with the station house on the south side. There were no coal drops here, but an open goods shed. In the 1950s the back of the yard was transformed by huge grain silos which were built here, visible for miles and used for collecting malting barley from farms around.

Heslerton (1m.1583yd.) was similar in configuration to Knapton, except for the additon of a single yard sidng to a coal drop on the north side. The signal box was odd in that it was turned sideways to face the rails end-on, with an entrance off the platform on its long side, steps up to a central door at operating level on the roadside and nameboard above it. A similar structure is to be found at Weaverthorpe. The station house on the south side had twin, high two storey gables. Yedingham and West Heslerton were a good mile equidistant on each side of the crossing.

C7 No. 2196 at Heaton shed in May 1938 *Photo: J.W. Hague*

D20 No. 2360 at Botanic Gardens

Weaverthorpe (3m. 774yd.) was a more thorough-going place with, firstly, a Down refuge siding, a three road goods yard opposite with goods shed and even a five ton crane, followed by the crossing, signal box and parallel platform with a usual type of station house on the south side. The siding with coal drop was similar to that at Heslerton, with a small dock at the platform end. The signal box, as said, was similarly oddly located at right angles and both had ticket racks to the rear of the structure. The station here was originally called Sherburn, after the nearest village to the south, however, this had to change, firstly and uselessly to Wykeham in 1874 until that village, miles away and unlinked by road received its own station on the Forge Valley line; then a place some five miles distant on the top of the Wolds was tried, Weaverthorpe, after old ladies found themselves at Sherburn-in-Elmet or, worse, Sherborne in Dorset!

Ganton (1m.1034 yd.) was slightly different in that a single Up siding came first with goods shed, then crossing with the signal box on the south side and parallel platforms with station house to the south. The yard of four roads was on the north side with two coal drops. Ganton village is small and pretty, a short way away on the A64. A refinement here is the golf course, once famous in Edwardian times. The station was probably more generously equipped than necessary because of the potential catchment area of the Filey district. The aforementioned goods shed was in fact a separate afterthought.

Seamer and the seaside

From Ganton the line curved north round Willerby Carr and Seamer Ings, crossing the Scarborough-Staxton road (A64) at Spittal Crossing (3m.18yd.) after minor crossings at Muston Drain, Pasture Lane and Meads Lane. Spittal faded when the trunk road was upgraded in 1936 and an overbridge was provided. Approaching Seamer, sand and gravel quarries could be seen at the side of the coast line from Filey which came in from the right, while to the left the Forge Valley single line came in; this closed in 1950 and was lifted beyond Thorton Dale in 1952. The Forge Valley line ran alongside in front of Seamer West box of 1906 (1m.604yd.) where the Filey line also joined and where points turned the former into a Down independent line, at the side of which a ticket platform was built for the inspection and collection of same. This replaced one which had been closed when Londesborough Road station was opened. In 1913 a public platform was built at Seamer station, further along, linked by a footbridge. Seamer itself was an oddity in that it was an island platform having assorted buildings which made standing on its narrowness rather perilous, covered by an open canopy at the crossing end on cast iron legs, which put one in mind of the old Hornby Gauge 'O' island platform accessory available for the train sets pre-war. On the right at the level crossing was Seamer East signal box (747yd.) which replaced an earlier 1873 cabin in 1913; both cabins continued to stand next to each other, the earlier one presumably retained for storage use until its demise in 1994. For all its drawbacks an island here would be very useful for changing purposes, with three routes involved. At the south end of the island was a form of extended crossover road which could at a pinch house a railcar for the Pickering line, while on the Up side were two very long sidings of 478yd. to cope with excursion overspills. Beyond the road crossing on the left was a small goods yard with coal drop and a line to the wooden goods shed. One reference mentions a 1 ton 10 cwt. crane here, though this is not shown elsewhere. Passengers would be fairly numerous, from Seamer village one mile away and the growing centres of Eastfield and Crossgates. To the east of the line at one time was a cattle auction market.

In view of the immense amount of traffic that developed, it was most surprising that the NER did not proceed to widen the route into Scarborough to provide four tracks, since both land and the powers to make use of it were available. From Seamer the run to the terminus might be better described in a sequence of the items passed en route. Firstly, close to Queen Margaret's road bridge was Weaponness (sometimes with one 'n') signal box (1m. 9yd.). At Mere Lane bridge matters became more active with the ten Gasworks Down sidings on the left, the gas works proper on the right and the signal box (1708yd.), and straight engine shed of eight roads on the left. This point marked the finish of the independent running lines on each side. To the right were five Gasworks Up sidings opposite the roundhouse shed left, with Washbeck signal box (473yd.) also on the left. To its rear was the Falsgrave coal depot. After Londesborough Road station, also on the left, to which latterly Whitby trains had been able to run to their own platform instead of reversing across the station layout, came Gallow's Close tunnel, left, of single track, and Falsgrave signal box (574yd.), now the sole survivor and at one time the control point for the management of station yard working and excursion information. Beyond here a train was within station limits when passing Central box (315yd.), closed on 22nd October 1984. A further coal depot was on view on the right hand side beyond the end platform.

Today the station looks superficially as it was, reduced to five platforms, two of which are in the open air, while the expanse of roof on the east side where the goods shed was at one time now covers a car park. Things are spick and span, however, and the delights of the town still beckon.

Train Services

An outline of train services now follows; it should be read in conjunction with the extracts from Bradshaw's timetable for various years, which are appended.

The Scarborough line began with a service of three trains each way per day, completing the journey in a little over two hours. In 1846, the following year, this was increased to three to York as well as a Monday early service to connect with a London train which would arrive on the same day. In summer there were five trains each way, while on Sundays there was a mail train and excursions. In December 1846 the service from Filey connected with three out of four of the York trains at Seamer. The Whitby service was also in full swing from 1850, with the York-Whitby service taking three hours, and that from Scarborough via Rillington 2 $^1/_2$ hours. Rillington suffered the ignominy of being regarded as on the Whitby route only, with only two York-Scarborough trains; the 6 am. ex York and 7.15 am. from Scarborough called there. One of the Down trains ran faster to York, in 1 hr. 40 mins.

Trains could now run through to Leeds, with one of the best the 10.45 am. from Scarborough which reached York in 1 hr . 15 min. then ran on to Leeds via Castleford, arriving there at 1 pm. An Act of 1838 obliged the railways to carry mail and newspapers, which was done on the first Down train reaching Scarborough at 9 am., and the last Up service.

Barton Hiill signal box in its later form, looking north. Photo: C.T. Goode

In 1852 the direct line to London via Peterborough was opened by the GNR, with first train from York, dep. 6 am., in summer, reaching the resort at 8 am. In 1862 the timing was advanced to 3.44 am., with a stop at Malton, to reach Scarborough at 5.10 am. This was followed by a slower mail which left York at 5.45 am. and halted everywhere. Eventually the time of the mail settled at 4.20 am. ex York until 1914, having a special sorting carriage. The mail did in fact survive until 1980. Cheap parliamentary fares of 1d. a mile were available on first and last trains, with market tickets at single fare for the return journey each Saturday morning from Malton to York. Fares were relatively expensive, with first, second and third from York to the following places as examples:

Castle Howard 3/6, 2/6 and 2/-. Malton 5/-, 3/6 and 2/6.

Scarborough 10/-, 7/- and 5/-. Whitby 12/-, 9/6 and 7/-.

Third Class was 1 1/2 d. per mile, while a day return was 1 1/2 times the single. One ray of light was that a day return taken on a Saturday was available homeward on Mondays.

A big railway development which affected the social and working lives of many was opening of the direct line from York to Leeds in 1872, bringing into being a new traveller, the commuter who was prepared to travel the seventy miles or so return each day. When he first tried out the principle, commuter-man could leave Scarborough at 8.20 am., arrive Leeds at 10.15 am. and return from Leeds at 5 pm. to arrive home at 7.05 pm. stopping at Malton both ways and Seamer on return. In fact the times were waiting to be improved and by the 1880s the fastest time between York and Scarborough had been reduced by five minutes to 65 minutes.

Years of make-do followed, though lavatories appeared on coaches in 1893 and new bogie vehicles from 1895, these made in York Works, under the eye of the General Manager, George Gibb, himself a commuter from Scarborough to York.

With improvement in locomotives from those of Tennant to Wilson Worsdell's handsome machines, things begin to hum a little more; in 1899 the Leeds-Scarborough run was reeled off in 1 hr. 45 min. with a non-stop 55 min. dash from York, though one of the Up trains performed the run in 50 min. On 1st June 1900 a non-stop summer expresss ran from Leeds to Scarborough in 75 min., carrying out the run from York, passed at 10 mph. to Scarborough in 42.5 min. at an average speed of 60 mph. which included the Howardian curves. Of course, the loads were often light, of four coaches or so; the engines were Worsdell's J Class 4-2-2- singles. The star performers were Nos. 1523/4 who regularly tackled the 27 mins. allowed between Leeds and York and the 48 mins. to Scarborough, providing fast runs of 73-77 mph. on the stretches from Micklefield to Church Fenton and Rillington to Ganton. The fastest runs were in the summer and in spite of calls made for the same to happen all the year round things remained the same. The fast through runs had extended to Bradford by 1914, the 8.20 am. ex Scarborough reaching Leeds at 9.40 am., Bradford (Midland) at 10.10 am., with a return at 4.45 pm., 5.13 pm. Leeds.

This was an early and unofficially named 'Scarborough Limited' of four coaches, as there was also a 'Scarborough Flier' (sic) which had been introduced from 1901. It had been possible to travel in some style from Scarborough to King's Cross from the 1850s, using the 'Flying Scotsman' at 10 am., changing at York and arriving at 6.05 pm. The Up service was not so exciting. From 1862 Scarborough could be reached at 4.45 pm. via Doncaster and Knottingley. Things improved once the direct NER line to Selby and Shaftholme Jc. opened, so that from 1886 the resort was available at 3.30 pm., including a half hour wait at York. At this time the Up service to London toook at least five hours.

From the turn of the century travel from King's Cross to Scarborough was quite reasonable, especially in the summer when a through train would leave the capital at 11.30 am. travelling through to the resort with a halt for an engine change in York and arriving there at 4.40 pm. This was, however, not as swift as taking a service which required a change in York, though it was convenient for those with piles of heavy luggage. The return service left Scarborough at 2.55 pm. and reached London at 8.30 pm. These services were retained on Fridays and Saturdays only until 1914. There was also a daily through service from King's Cross at 1.05 pm., reaching Scarborough just before 6 pm. on which lunches were served.

Through coaches were minor irritants, particularly to York Operating department who had to find, often at short notice, trains to which to attach them if they turned up out of the blue, as did happen, then sending them on to Scarborough where the platforms were not long enough to hold the length. Trains were often duplicated at short notice if stock were available. The LNWR were dabs at running through coaches; one delightful working ran from that company's little station in Oxford to Bletchley, then Northampton, Market Harborough, Melton Mowbray, Newark and thence via the GN main line. Other companies favoured direct running by their own trains, which the NER encouraged, such as a through GC service out of Marylebone at 8.15 am., arriving Scarborough at 2.45 pm. The MR sought to compete and brought along trains, often from obscure mining areas such as Doe Hill, headed by small, valiant 4F good engines.

From 1923 the new LNER strove to make Scarborough attractive to Londoners and put on a service dep. King's Cross at 11.50 am. which took 3 $^1/_2$ hours for the 188 m. to York, a record for rail travel at the time, to reach the resort at 4.20 pm. in 4 $^1/_2$ hours. The return trip left the resort at 3 pm. and took exactly the same time on the way back. In 1933 the non-stop portion of the run to York was cut to 3 $^1/_4$ hr., then to 3 hr. in 1935 with 50 min. allowed from York to Scarborough and 5 min. engine change in York, quite a feat in itself. The London-Scarborough run had now come down to 3 hrs. 55 min. for a stretch of 230.2 miles. Often streamlined A4 'Pacifics' would be used as far as York with D49s or perhaps a C7 'Atlantic' in charge to Scarborough. A Whitby Composite First/Third coach ran north next to the engine, was detached at York with the train engine and put on the 2.15 pm. which called at Pickering, Goathland and Grosmont to reach Whitby at 3.15 pm., all very civilised. The Up service left Scarborough at 10.40 am., arrive York at 11.30 am. where it attached the Whitby vehicle (dep. 9.40 am.) to reach London with the eleven coach train at 2.35 pm. On summer Saturdays a relief train left ten minutes before the main service, also non-stop to York and reaching Scarborough at 3.07 pm. Meanwhile, the service proper, following a slightly easier schedule, reached Scarborough at 3.15 pm. Whitby also had a non-stop express of its own, leaving King's Cross at 11.25 am. and shedding a through coach to Bridlington at Selby (unadvertised). Whitby was gained at 4.30 pm. The parade, of course, also took place in the Up direction.

The MR and GC competed for the growing commuter traffic to Sheffield, the NER favouring the MR as the two had constructed a joint line from York through Pontefract into South Yorks. Thus, in 1901 the 8.35 am. from Scarborough would arrive at Sheffield Midland at 10.36 am., while the 4.42 pm. would reach Scarborough at 6.55 pm. The GC, never to be out-gunned, came up with some fast running over its route via Filey and Bridlington, the 8.30 am. departure arr. Sheffield Victoria at 10.30 am., with a return at 4.35 pm. reaching Scarborough at 7 pm. A comparison with the Midland times above is interesting.

Then there were all the charter and public excursions, sometimes duplicated, all of which had to be dispersed at Scarborough for collection later. The pilot would take out the empty stock, leaving the train engine to emerge from the buffers and wait for instructions to move the empty vehicles of the next. This was fine, unless the train crew was obstinate or tired out or just knew little of the layout they had arrived in and cared even less. Most excursions ran to platform 1 and could be cleared on a ten minute headway. Those to Londesborough Road were drawn ahead through the tunnel to Gallows Close, where they were away from the hurly-burly.

The local workings ran as usual in the midst of the summer turmoil, with some exspansion at the York end due to developments in housing at Haxby and Strensall, catered for by a new generation of rail moter. Of the country stations, Knapton and Kirkham had the least booked passengers, though the latter would have more arrivals from excursions. Haxby was busy, with 21,000, as was Strensall with 30,000; this could be double in wartime due to the military presence. Weaverthorpe, oddly, was busy, with nearly 11,000 over the same period. Problems arose with the growth of road transport, when railway companies could buy shares in bus companies, and then reduce or abolish country branch lines. In the case in question the LNER had interests in both the United and West Yorkshire buses from 1928 and it was this which caused the local Scarborough line stations to close from 22nd September 1930, leaving however, their options open with platforms in position, even though the signal boxes were only 'switched in when required'.

The Motive Power

West Yorkshire buses ran excursions from York station to Castle Howard, while United provided popular half day tours to the Forge Valley from Scarborough. After the Depression of 1932 there was a revival of Sunday excursions and penny-a-mile fares. A very popular run was the scenic excursion which ran from Scarborough or Hull to Malton, Pickering and Whitby, the Hull route being taken tender first from Driffield to Malton, on one occasion with a Dairycoates based J23 from the old H & BR. These engines managed to break into the NER scheme of things after Grouping fairly easily, as the H & B had been absorbed by the NER the year before. One of the engines was housed at Scarborough, another at Pickering and four at Whitby, proving their worth on the tougher stretches of route. The universal workhorse, however, was the B16 4-6-0 developed from the earlier B15 and available at Scarborough for use on mixed traffic, excursions, fast goods and mineral workings. No. 845 was resident from January 1930 to 1943 for all these duties, including the coal runs from Gascoigne Wood yard, and host to the many visiting B16s which appeared in the summer. The engine was the first to be scrapped in 1958 as No. 61474. During the war all the B16s were for a time shedded at York to centralise the maintenance and swap spares. Afterwards some dispersal took place, though clusters remained, as in 1952: York 35, Neville Hill (Leeds) 33, Scarborough 1 and Dairycoates 8. At the latter place the 9.05 am. Hull-Scarborough ran at several times in up to five duplicates of ten coaches hauled by B16s, while Neville Hill called out some of its own stud to haul duplicates of its expresses to the coast of up to twelve coaches, these being evening outings.

It was not unknown for a B16 to enjoy a run with 'The Scarborough Flyer' in 1957.

The 4-4-0s were the important passenger engines around Scarborough for compactness and strength, often types which had been 'cascaded down' from more important work elsewhere by more modern classes. Thus, after the Class J singles mentioned earlier came the early 4-4-0s of LNER Class D22 and 23 with four at Scarborough in 1923 (Nos. 356,779,1541/2) and one at Malton in 1926, as well as a D23 at Malton between 1923 and 28. The D17s were a class of handsome racers with 7 ft. driving wheels covered by a single splasher, one of which, No

1621 is happily preserved. In 1923 six were at Scarborough and No. 1902 was there from 1939-43 in use as an air raid shelter with a defence of sand bags! Best of all the Worsdell offerings were the D20s, which proved to be thoroughly reliable in service, even in the rigours of wartime. In 1927 and 1935 four were at Scarborough, with three there in 1939 and 1947. At this time Selby, a roundhouse shed, had two in 1935, seven in 1939 and nine in 1947, often using one to replace a steam railcar and in tandem on heavy expresses in summertime. Incidentally the Doncaster-York morning stopping train via Selby was extended to the Foss Islands branch to serve Rowntree's halt - a D20 turn.

Of Vincent Raven's 'Atlantics' in LNER Classes C6 and C7, the former were older, rougher riding and heavier on coal, but were loved by the drivers who could keep heavy loads moving with the engine at a brisk pace. Twenty were built and sent to the chief NER depots, as seven were to Gateshead. In 1939 the last two remaining there were sent to Scarborough, together with four from York, but were little used, being too long for the turntable. Bridlington managed six which fared better for workings and attention.

Flaxton signal box with older gates *Photo: C.T. Goode*

At the reshuffle of classes into bigger clusters on 28th March 1943 the C6s were retained by Gateshead, Dairycoates (Hull) getting two, with ten most surprisingly going to Springhead and, perhaps even worse for them, two out to far-flung Cudworth on the Hull & Barnsley, hardly the sort of environment for them. In August 1946 the last three were to be found at Dairycoates, the final, (No. 2933) departing from there in March 1948. If used at all, the class during wartime would have pottered about the goods yards, often with traces of green livery beneath the rust and grime and gusts of steam which leaked from every fissure.

The fifty younger C7s went to Tyneside (30) and York, Leeds and Haymarket (20). The first venture by the class coastwards was by No. 732, which was fitted with Lentz poppet valves; it had left Gateshead in February 1934 for York, moving to the resort from there in March 1945. At that date eight C7s went to Scarborough from Dairycoates, where the shed foreman was probably delighted to be rid of them as he had been given 22 of them in March 1943.

By December 1947 there were still five C7s at Scarborough, for which there were three turns, the first a round trip to Leeds and back in the morning and a round trip to York in the afternoon, the second down to Hull and back in the morning with an evening outing to York, while the third, which one hardly dares to mention, was the round trip to Gascoigne Wood for the coal traffic.

No. 2970 (2164) was the last to be scrapped from Dairycoates on 27th December 1947.

Like the later B1s, the Gresley D49s, named after Hunts and Shires made a radical impact on the current incumbents of the engine sheds, with Scarborough receiving six, some brand new in the mid 1930s and retaining five between 1939 and June 1953. Soon an efficient pattern was set up on the Leeds-Scarborough trains, an allowance of 30 min. being for the 25 $^{1}/_{2}$m. Leeds to York, increased by five minutes during wartime with trains of 7 or 8 vehicles. Rough riding did become a problem, with the D49s after a period in service, requiring a careful approach at pointwork around York in particular. From 1955 onwards the engines had humbler tasks working goods and coal trains, the Gascoigne Wood run included. This was not unusual at this time; once proud Gresley 'Pacifics' could be found on pick-up goods and trains of empties, and the newer B1s found themselves on very menial jobs. No. 274 'The Craven' spent several years at Scarborough, while the last in traffic were Nos. 62711/29 'Dumbartonshire' and 'Rutlandshire' until 1st May 1961.

Clearance of the older, smaller types, the G5-4 0-4-4Ts, J72 shunters, A8 4-6-2Ts for the Whitby line and NER goods 0-6-0s such as the J24s (three apiece at Whitby and Malton in 1947) went on steadily as the B1 4-6-0s of Thompson's efficient design came along and were more and more ubiquitous. Hull's No. 61010 'Wildebeeste' for instance managed to run the scenic excurion at various times in its life as well as the pick-up goods to Bridlington. The newer ones did in fact become more and more unkempt as new diesel power arrived which needed less care, but still managed to bring holiday excursions until well into the 60s. However, it was all to end very quickly once the dieselisation programme swung into action.

Diesel multiple units came first to the Bradford, Leeds, Harrogate and Knaresborough lines in June 1954, when revenue soared to 400%. The ride, views and timekeeping were all superb. Steam did keep coming along on excursions until 1967, even though the dmus had been in action at Scarborough since 7th March 1960. The steam shed closed on 22nd May 1963, though the yard and its facilities were still available. Between York and Scarborough the best running time was now 53 min., though the overall time from Leeds was 8 min. slower. In 1950 the 'Scarborough Flyer' returned after a long absence, down Friday and Saturday, back Saturday and Sunday, its running time up by 33 min. with two engine changes at Grantham and York; additionally the motive power on the Scarborough section was decidedly rough at times. The swan song for excursions was in 1959, when nearly a million passengers came to Scarborough and rolling stock was stored all the way back to Strensall. A pick-up goods still left Gallows Close at this time, and an express goods-cum-fish left the town each weekday at 6.40 pm.

Londesborough Road station closed on 4th July 1966, the last departure being the 2.35 pm. to Basford on 24th August 1963.

For a time the new dmus were based at Hull Springhead, the least used of the engine sheds at the time, to allow new crews to familiarise themselves with routines and to iron out any potential difficulties. Cravens units Nos. 50359 and 56114 ran to Scarborough on trial trips on 11th and 12th September 1956, out express and returning as a stopping service, with the reverse happening on 17th and 18th. On 25th and 27th of the same month an XP van was attached for weight and loading tests. This feature was to appear in due course during the heavy period of Christmas mail.

One operational snippet is of interest. On Saturday, 6th October 1956 the 8.35 am. Scarborough-York pick-up derailed two wagons at Weaverthorpe, blocking both running lines for some time. This caused the 10.20 am. Scarborough-York to be diverted via Filey, Bridlington and Market Weighton, a longer but much more scenic route. This missed the Malton stop for the transfer of Whitby passengers. The 10.36 am. Scarborough-Blackpool excursion managed to pass the derailment on the wrong line and carried the Whitby passengers who were able to leave the train at Rillington, where a special stop was made, and where the Malton-Whitby service also made a special halt for them. Thus Rillington had its further moment of glory, presumably because it was likely to cause less fuss than bothering to halt the train at Malton.

One of the fussy signal gantries at the approach to Scarborough, with the original turntable in the foreground serving the old roundhouse off left. The castle is visible in the background. *Photo: C.T. Goode*

Further Railway Schemes - at Haxby

There were three minor railways which were planned - one even executed - in the wake of the major development in the Malton area. Incentives were the development of the internal combustion engine and the interest of such enthusiasts as Col. Stephens in promoting light railways which did not require such stringent rules for their safety and operation as did 'big brother' and which could be laid with light materials on the surface of the land without too many tunnels and bridges. Farmers not directly connected to the main line by stations sought outlets for their products by promoting new, light railways, while owners of sand and gravel pits and peat works wished to link their premises to some convenient railhead in order to disperse their wares. Already, then, in the York area the Easingwold Railway, a short affair off the main line at Alne had arrived to please the farmers (and its promoters), while the Derwent Valley Light Railway mentioned here earlier had been successful at the same time as our two failed contenders with its weedy line through Dunnington and Wheldrake to Selby (almost).

Turning the camera south from the same spot as the previous picture more signals can be seen and the Gasworks signal box, with newer engine shed behind a large heap of coal

Photo: C.T. Goode

The first proposal was by a farm consortium, the Brandsby Co-operative Society, in 1912 for a Haxby & Brandsby Light Railway which would run from a junction at Haxby station northwards for nine miles, with stations east of Sutton-on-Forest and Stillington. Halts would be provided at Suet Carr and Marton. The terminus would be set in a field south of the Stillington and Brandsby road. The gauge would be standard, with passengers changing at Haxby and goods working through, presumably using the parent company's wagons. Seven miles of the line would be level, with 1 $^1/_4$ m. at 1 in 100 and only $^1/_4$ m. at 1 in 50 rising before Brandsby.

Promoters of the line were Mr. Fairfax Cholmeley of Brandsby, farming 3,000 acres, Mrs. Rowntree, also of Brandsby and a Mr. Horner of York. There was vigorous opposition from the Easingwold Railway people who had been advised that their running costs could be undercut by £3 per mile by the new railway which served an area hitherto uncovered. At Sutton, for instance, milk was sent to York by road regularly at an exorbitant price, as no direct railhead was available. The Easingwold faction put forward a counter scheme which would extend its 2 $^1/_2$ mile line down through Stillington to Farlington and Sheriff Hutton. It already ran nine passenger services a day, with a paltry yearly profit of £2,358. The new line from Haxby would have a 'pendulating' service of three trains daily, perhaps more in keeping with Brandsby's population of a mere 324. The enthusiasm and finance were both present, but wartime intervened and plans were shelved, happy though the prospects were.

- at Burythorpe.

The Light Railway Commissioners met the promoters of the Burythorpe Light Railway at Malton Town Hall on 22nd July 1913; here was a different sort of railway, sponsored by men of larger vision and ideas, for sand was involved, white sand used for steel and glass making. Of course, the scheme was also to accommodate agricultural produce and a few passengers, as well as sweeten the farming orders. Promoters were Mr. C. Paley Scott and Mr. J.H. Preston of Burythorpe House, on whose land the sand deposits lay. Norton RDC were in favour of the project, and there was only one dissenter, a Mr. Holmes who found that the line would be passing between his farm buildings and his fields.

The line was to be of two foot gauge, single and worked by small oil engines of 12-15 hp. capable of hauling 15 bottom emptying trucks. A speed limit of 10 mph. would be set, though 6 mph. would be expected. There would be four stations along the 2m . 2 furlong route, starting from a transit platform at Huttons Ambo station, then across the river to a halt at Laysike, next How Beck at 6 $^1/_2$ furlongs, Eddlethorpe near the crossing of an early Roman road, to end at Burythorpe. There would be six road crossings and the area served would be roughly 9,000 acres. A chief feature would be the bridge crossing the Derwent, spanning 90 ft. with lattice girders, 8 ft. wide and, unusually of two decks, the lower with 15 ft. headroom taking a bridleway for animals and carts, for which a toll of 1/- return would be levied for man and horse, 2d. for a cow and 'less' for a sheep. Trains would not be allowed to pass over the bridge at the same time as cattle, to avoid disturbance caused by rumbling. Both road and railway would have been a real boon to villagers generally, as the only means of crossing the Derwent were the bridges at Kirkham and Malton some distance away. Considering this, it was decided to fix a higher rate for carriage than normal, at 27% above the usual level; the bulk of this would fall to the sand company. No mention is made of passenger rolling stock. The line would fall to the river, levelling out on the bridge, then down to Laysike at 1 in 26 with a final average rise at 1 in 65. The bridge sounded a bargain with an estimate, queried at the meeting of £600.

The council pointed out that the sand was currently conveyed by steam wagon at the rate of 3,000 tons yearly for three miles along a road which was in places only ten feet wide and also steep, causing much wear and tear. A new wheel had cost £40, while wear to the road cost up to 2/3d. per ton load. Mr. Barton Kilner, of preserving jar repute, bottle manufacturer of Wakefield, stated that he could take as much of the sand as could be sent to him. His firm had taken up to 5,000 tons in the past and thought that the material was the best in England and was 'too good for bottle making.' Any competition in this field came from the Belgian direction, so that the railway needed to move the sand at Burythorpe at a proper profit. The Vicar of Acklam suggested that some agricultural land was reverting to gravel and scrub, as farmers were unwilling to cultivate it, leaving labourers'cottages also out of use.

Capital to be raised for the line was £25,000, with all shares held by the same company. Again, alas, war intervened and the project failed, though one voice at the meeting did declare rather weakly that the bridge alone would seem to provide all the advantages required without a light tramway.

Mr Paxton of Laysike House, wrote a somewhat cynical letter about the above line. He pointed out that, as the line was to carry sand, then of course it would pay, but if it were continued to Burythorpe village, only then would it be seen whether passengers would appear. Some he had met wished to extend the run to Acklam and Leavening, though he had heard farmers say, on the other hand, that they would continue to ride horses to travel to Malton instead of leaving them idle in stables. There would always be Saturday shoppers, or perhaps a couple might come out for a jaunt to look at the 'thorpes' on a Thursday afternoon. He thought that the meeting should have decided 'we do not want to carry passengers unless we are compelled.' There were folk who suggested that Burythorpe could become the centre of a bottle manufactury. This would be next to impossible without a handy supply of coal, up to a thousand workers and housing and belching chimneys which that would bring. He too, welcomed the Derwent bridge proposal.

- and Sand Hutton

The final scheme was seen to work, for a time at least, though not quite in the same rank as the above, not directly linked to our main line, and not in the same spirit. In 1912 Sir Robert Walker of Sand Hutton Hall, a good way south of Flaxton, floated a 15 in. gauge pleasure railway which ran north from the station at Warthill on the York-Hull line through his estate with halts at the Hall, gardens, alongside the road to the village, then north with one branch (goods) to Claxton and the other to Bossall, which brings us into the same district as Burythorpe a short way from Barton Hill station. Thus some affinity can be claimed. The outfit was changed in 1922 to an 18 in. line to carry passengers and freight, though how much of each is hard to fathom; certainly details of facilities appeared in the Railway Clearing House handbooks of the day. The line closed on 30th June 1932, two years after the owner's death at the early age of 39.

Another largish gantry at the platform ends of Scarborough
Photo: C.T. Goode

A group of signals serving the excursion platforms at Falsgrave.
Photo: C.T. Goode

Gallows Close signal box looking north, with the Whitby line in the foreground curving away right under Wykeham Road bridge.

Photo: C.T. Goode

Sand Hutton Light Railway. July 1925

Miles			S	S	S	W
0	Bossall		8.05	12.20	4.30	8.05
1 1/4	Kissthorne		8.20	12.35	4.45	8.20
1 3/4	Memorial		8.25	12.40	4.50	8.25
2 1/2	Sand Hutton Cen.		8.30	12.45	4.55	8.30
4 1/2	Warthill	arrv.	8.45	1.00	5.10	8.45

		S	A	S
Warthill		1.05	3.05	5.18
Sand Hutton Cen.		1.20	3.20	5.30
Memorial		1.25	3.25	5.35
Kissthorne		1.30	3.30	5.40
Bossall	arrv.	1.40	3.45	5.55

By July 1929 the service was two trains on Sats only leaving Bossall at 12.15 pm. and 4.30, and three from Warthill on Sats only at 1.05 pm., 3.15 and 5.25.

S: Sats. Only. W: Weds. Only. A: Wed. & Sats Only

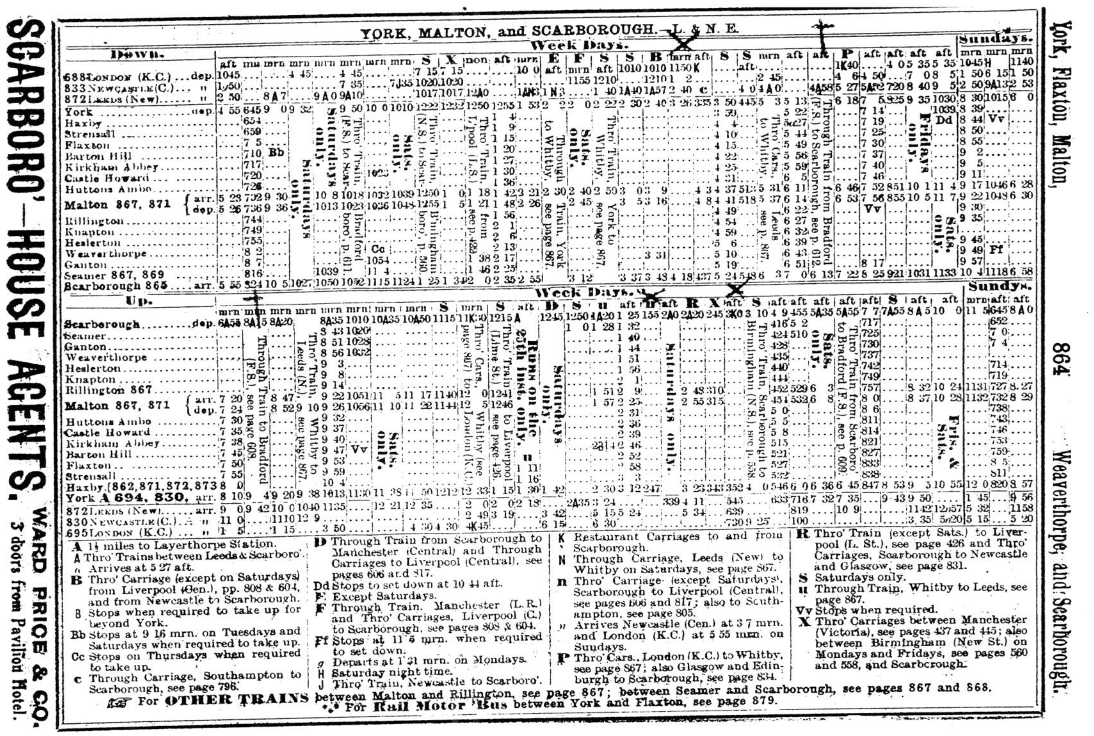

YORK, MALTON, and SCARBOROUGH.—L. & N. E.

Down. — Week Days.

Down.	aft	mrn	mrn	mrn	mrn	mrn	mrn	mrn	S	X	non	aft
688 London (K.C.) ...dep.	1045	...	...	4 45	...	4 45	...	...	7 15	7 15	...	...
833 Newcastle (C.) ... "	1 50	...	...	...	...	7 35	...	7J35	1020	1020	...	...
872 Leeds (New) ...... "	2 50	...	8A7	...	9A0	9A10	...	...	1017	1017	12A0	...
York ...dep.	4 55	645	9 0	9 32		9 50	10 0	1010	1222	1232	1250	1255
Haxby	...	654	...				...			...		1 4
Strensall	...	659	...				...			...		1 9
Flaxton	...	7 5	...				...			...		1 15
Barton Hill	...	710	Bb				...			...		1 20
Kirkham Abbey	...	717	...				...			...		1 27
Castle Howard	...	720	...				1023			...		1 30
Huttons Ambo	...	726	...				...			...		1 36
Malton 867, 871 arr.	5 23	732	9 30		10 8	1018	1032	1039	1250	1 0	1 18	1 42
Malton 867, 871 dep.	5 26	736	9 36		1013	1023	1036	1048	1255	1 5	1 21	1 48
Rillington	...	744	...				...	...		...		1 56
Knapton	...	749	...				...	...		...		2 1
Heslerton	...	755	...				...	...		...		2 6
Weaverthorpe	...	8 2	...				Cc	...		...		2 13
Ganton	...	8 7	...				1054	...		...	1 38	2 17
Seamer 867, 869	...	816	...		1039		11 4	...		...	1 46	2 25
Scarborough 865 ...arr.	5 55	824	10 5	1027	1050	1052	1115	1124	1 25	1 34	2 0	2 35
Notes				Saturdays only.	Saturdays only.	Thro' Train, (F.S.) to Scar-boro', Bradford p. 611.		Sats. only.	Thro' Train, B'mingham (N.S.) to Scar-boro', p. 560.		Thro' Train, from L'pool (L.S.) see p. 422.	

Down.	mrn	E aft	F mrn	S aft	S	B	mrn	aft K	S	S aft	mrn	aft
688 London (K.C.) ...dep.	10 0				1010	1010	1150		...			...
833 Newcastle (C.) ... "	...	...	1155	1210	...	1210	1 2		...		2 45	...
872 Leeds (New) ...... "	1AN3	1 N3	...	1 40	1A40	1A57	2 40	c	...	4 0	4A0	...
York ...dep.	1 53	2 2	2 0	2 22	2 30	2 40	3 26	3 35	3 50	4 45	5 3	5 13
Haxby	...		...		...	...	...	...	3 59	...		5 22
Strensall	...		...		...	...	...	...	4 4	...		5 27
Flaxton	...		...		...	...	...	...	4 10	...		5 44
Barton Hill	...		...		...	...	...	...	4 15	...		5 49
Kirkham Abbey	...		...		...	...	...	...	4 22	...		5 56
Castle Howard	...		...		...	...	...	...	4 25	...		5 59
Huttons Ambo	...		...		...	...	...	...	4 31	...		6 5
Malton 867, 871 arr.	2 21	2 30	2 40	2 50	3 0	3 9	...	4 3	4 37	5 13	5 31	6 11
Malton 867, 871 dep.	2 26		2 45		3 5	3 16	...	4 8	4 41	5 18	5 37	6 14
Rillington	...		...		...	...	...	...	4 49			6 22
Knapton	...		...		...	...	...	...	4 54			6 27
Heslerton	...		...		...	...	...	...	4 59			6 32
Weaverthorpe	...		...		...	...	...	...	5 6			6 39
Ganton	...		...		...	3 31	...	...	5 10			6 43
Seamer 867, 869	...		...		...	...	...	...	5 19			6 51
Scarborough 865 ...arr.	2 55		3 12		3 37	3 48	4 18	4 27	5 24	5 48	6 3	7 0
Notes		Through Train, York to Whitby, see page 867.	Sats. only.	Thro' Train, York to Whitby, see page 867.							Thro' Cars., Leeds to Whitby, see p. 867.	

Down.	aft	P aft	aft	aft	aft	aft	Sundays. mrn	mrn	mrn
688 London (K.C.) ...dep.	...	1K40	...	4 0	5 35	5 35	1045	H	1140
833 Newcastle (C.) ... "	...	4 6	4 50	...	7 0	8 5	1 50	6 15	1 50
872 Leeds (New) ...... "	4A58	5 27	5A52	720	8 40	9 5	2 50	9A13	2 53
York ...dep.		6 18	7 5	8 25	9 35	1030	8 30	1015	6 0
Haxby		...	7 14	...		1039	8 39	...	...
Strensall		...	7 19	...		Dd	8 44	Vv	...
Flaxton		...	7 25	...		...	8 50	...	...
Barton Hill		...	7 30	...		...	8 55	...	...
Kirkham Abbey		...	7 37	...		...	9 2	...	...
Castle Howard		...	7 40	...		...	9 5	...	...
Huttons Ambo		...	7 46	...		...	9 11	...	...
Malton 867, 871 arr.		6 46	7 52	851	10 1	11 4	9 17	1046	6 28
Malton 867, 871 dep.		6 53	7 56	855	10 5	11 7	9 22	1048	6 30
Rillington		...	Vv	...	...		9 30	...	...
Knapton		...	...	...	...		9 35	...	...
Heslerton		...	...	...	...		...	...	...
Weaverthorpe		...	...	...	...		9 45	...	...
Ganton		...	...	...	...		9 49	Ff	...
Seamer 867, 869		...	8 17	...	...		9 57	...	...
Scarborough 865 ...arr.	6 13	7 22	8 25	921	1031	1133	10 4	1118	6 58
Notes	Through Train from Bradford (F.S.) to Scarborough, see p. 612.				Fridays only.	Sats. only.			

Up. — Week Days.

Up.	mrn	mrn	mrn	mrn	mrn	mrn	mrn	mrn	S	mrn	S
Scarborough ...dep.	6A55	8A15	8A20		8A35	1010	10A35	10A50	1115	11K30	1215 A
Seamer	...		...		8 43	1020		...	...		
Ganton	...		...		8 51	1028		...	...		
Weaverthorpe	...		...		8 56	1032		...	...		
Heslerton	...		...		9 3	...		...	...		
Knapton	...		...		9 8	...		...	...		
Rillington 867	...		...		9 14	...		...	...		
Malton 867, 871 arr.	7 20		8 47		9 22	1051	11 5	11 17	1140	12 0	1241
Malton 867, 871 dep.	7 24		8 52	9 10	9 26	1056	11 10	11 22	1144	12 5	1246
Huttons Ambo	7 30		...		9 32	...		...	...		
Castle Howard	7 35		...		9 37	...		...	...		
Kirkham Abbey	7 38		...		9 40	...		...	...		
Barton Hill	7 45		...		9 47	Vv		...	...		
Flaxton	7 50		...		9 53	...		...	...		
Strensall	7 55		...		9 59	...		...	...		
Haxby [862, 871, 872, 873	8 0		...		10 4	...		...	...		
York A 694, 830, arr.	8 10	9 4	9 20	9 38	1013	1130	11 38	11 50	1212	12 33	1 15
872 Leeds (New) ...arr.	9 0	9 42	10 0	1040	1135	...	12 21	12 35	...	2 0	2 0
830 Newcastle (C.) ... "	11 0	...	1110	12 9	...	...	...	...	...	2 49	3 19
695 London (K.C.) ... "	1 5	...	1 15	...	3 50	...	...	4 30	4 30	4K45	...
Notes		Through Train to Bradford (F.S.), see page 608.		Thro' Train, Whitby to Leeds (N.), see page 867.			Sats. only.			Thro' Cars., Whitby (see page 867) to London (K.C.)	Thro' Train to Liverpool (Lime St.) see page 426.

Up.	aft	D	S	u	aft	H aft	aft	R	X	aft
Scarborough ...dep.		1245	1250	1A20	1 25	155	2A0	2A20	245	3K0
Seamer			1 0	1 28	1 32	...		...	...	...
Ganton			...	...	1 40	...		...	...	...
Weaverthorpe			...	...	1 44	...		...	...	...
Heslerton			...	...	1 51	...		...	...	...
Knapton			...	...	1 56	...		...	...	...
Rillington 867			...	...	2 1	...		...	...	...
Malton 867, 871 arr.			...	1 51	2 9	...		2 48	310	...
Malton 867, 871 dep.			...	1 57	2 25	...		2 55	315	...
Huttons Ambo			...	...	2 31	...		...	...	...
Castle Howard			...	...	2 36	...		...	...	...
Kirkham Abbey			...	2 14	2 39	...		...	...	...
Barton Hill	u		...	...	2 46	...		...	...	...
Flaxton	1 11		...	...	2 52	...		...	...	...
Strensall	1 16		...	...	2 58	...		...	...	...
Haxby [862, 871, 872, 873	...		...	...	3 3	...		...	...	...
York A 694, 830, arr.	1 30	1 42	...	2 30	3 12	2 47		3 23	343	352
872 Leeds (New) ...arr.	2 18	...	2A35	3 24	...	...	339	4 11	...	545
830 Newcastle (C.) ... "	...	3 42	...	5 15	5 24	...	...	5 34	...	639
695 London (K.C.) ... "	...	6 15	...	6 30	...	...	...	...	...	730
Notes	Runs on the 25th inst. only.	Saturdays only.					Saturdays only.			

Up.	S	aft	aft	aft	aft	aft	S	aft	aft	Sundays. mrn	aft	aft
Scarborough ...dep.	3 10	4 9	455	5A35	5A55	7 7	7A55	8A5	10 0	11 5	645	8A0
Seamer		416	5 2			717	...	...	...	...	652	...
Ganton		424	510			725	...	...	...	...	7 0	...
Weaverthorpe		428	...			730	...	...	...	...	7 4	...
Heslerton		435	...			737	...	...	...	...	...	...
Knapton		440	...			742	...	...	...	...	714	...
Rillington 867		444	...			749	...	...	...	...	719	...
Malton 867, 871 arr.		452	529	6 3		757	...	8 32	10 24	1131	727	8 27
Malton 867, 871 dep.		454	532	6 8		8 0	...	8 37	10 28	1132	732	8 29
Huttons Ambo		5 0	...			8 6	...	...		...	738	...
Castle Howard		5 5	...			811	...	...		...	743	...
Kirkham Abbey		5 8	...			814	...	...		...	746	...
Barton Hill		515	...			821	...	...		...	753	...
Flaxton		521	...			827	...	...		...	759	...
Strensall		527	...			833	...	...		...	8 5	...
Haxby [862, 871, 872, 873		532	...			838	...	...		...	811	...
York A 694, 830, arr.	4 0	546	6 0	6 36	6 45	847	8 53	9 5	10 55	12 0	820	8 57
872 Leeds (New) ...arr.	...	633	716	7 32	7 35	...	9 43	9 50	...	1 45	...	9 56
830 Newcastle (C.) ... "	...	...	819	...	10 9	...	...	1142	12n57	5 32	...	1158
695 London (K.C.) ... "	9 25	...	100	...	...	...	...	3 35	5n20	5 15	...	5 20
Notes	Thro' Train, Scarborough to Birmingham (N.S.), see p. 558.			Sats. only.	Thro' Train from Scarboro' to Bradford (F.S.), see p. 609.				Fris. & Sats.			

A 1¼ miles to Layerthorpe Station.
A Thro' Trains between Leeds & Scarboro'.
a Arrives at 5 27 aft.
B Thro' Carriage (except on Saturdays) from Liverpool (Cen.), pp. 808 & 604, and from Newcastle to Scarborough.
B Stops when required to take up for beyond York.
Bb Stops at 9 16 mrn. on Tuesdays and Saturdays when required to take up.
Cc Stops on Thursdays when required to take up.
c Through Carriage, Southampton to Scarborough, see page 796.
D Through Train from Scarborough to Manchester (Central) and Through Carriages to Liverpool (Central), see pages 606 and 817.
Dd Stops to set down at 10 44 aft.
E Except Saturdays.
F Through Train, Manchester (L.R.) and Thro' Carriages, Liverpool (C.) to Scarborough, see pages 808 & 604.
Ff Stops at 11 5 mrn. when required to set down.
g Departs at 1 31 mrn. on Mondays.
H Saturday night time.
J Thro' Train, Newcastle to Scarboro'.
K Restaurant Carriages to and from Scarborough.
N Through Carriage, Leeds (New) to Whitby on Saturdays, see page 867.
n Thro' Carriage (except Saturdays), Scarborough to Liverpool (Central), see pages 606 and 817; also to Southampton, see page 805.
n Arrives Newcastle (Cen.) at 3 7 mrn. and London (K.C.) at 5 55 mrn. on Sundays.
P Thro' Cars., London (K.C.) to Whitby, see page 867; also Glasgow and Edinburgh to Scarborough, see page 834.
R Thro' Train (except Sats.) to Liverpool (L. St.), see page 426 and Thro' Carriages, Scarborough to Newcastle and Glasgow, see page 831.
S Saturdays only.
u Through Train, Whitby to Leeds, see page 867.
Vv Stops when required.
X Thro' Carriages between Manchester (Victoria), see pages 437 and 445; also between Birmingham (New St.) on Mondays and Fridays, see pages 560 and 558, and Scarborough.

☞ For **OTHER TRAINS** between Malton and Rillington, see page 867; between Seamer and Scarborough, see pages 867 and 868.
⁂ For **Rail Motor 'Bus** between York and Flaxton, see page 879.

Bradshaws July 1925

YORK, MALTON, PICKERING, WHITBY, and SCARBRO'.—North Eastern.

Miles from York	Single 1 cl. s. d.	Single 2 cl. s. d.	Single 3 cl. s. d.	Return 1 cl. s. d.	Return 2 cl. s. d.	Return 3 cl. s. d.	Down. New Station,	Week Days mrn	mrn	exp	mrn	exp	aft	exp	aft	exp	aft	Sndys mrn
							Leeds 362 ....dep.	2 14	7 25	9 5	11 0	1 35	1 35	3 30	3 30	5 30	6 55	2 14
							362 Normanton ... "	2 49	7 15	9 8	1150	1 5	1 5	3 15	3 15	5 29	6 54	2 49
							York ....dep.	5 15	8 40	10 2	1 0	2 30	3 30	4 47	5 0	6 30	7 50	5 5
4½	0 8	0 7	0 4				Haxby	5 25	8 50		1 10		3 40		5 10		8 0	5 15
6½	1 0	0 10	0 6½				Strensall	5 30	8 55		1 15		3 45		5 15		8 5	5 20
9	1 4	1 2	0 9				Flaxton	5 36	9 1		1 21		3 51		5 21		8 11	5 26
11½	1 7	1 4	0 11½				Barton Hill	5 41	9 6		1 26		3 56		5 26		8 16	5 31
15	2 0	1 8	1 3				Kirkham Abbey	5 48	9 15		1 35		4 5		5 35		8 25	5 40
15¾	2 2	1 10	1 3½				Castle Howard	5 51	9 18		1 38		4 8		5 38		8 28	5 43
18¼	2 6	2 1	1 6½				Huttons Ambo	5 58	9 24		1 44		4 14		5 44		8 34	5 49
21	2 11	2 5	1 9				**Malton 381, 375** ..arr.	6 4	9 30	1034	1 50	3 2	4 20	5 19	5 50	7 2	8 40	5 55
—							Scarbro' ....dep.	6 45	9 20	9 20	1 30		3 55				7 0	
—							*Whitby Branch.* **Malton** ....dep.	7 20	10 7	1040	2 10		4 35				8 50	6 10
25¼	3 6	2 11	2 1½				Rillington Junction	7 29	1016	1049	2 19		4 44				8 59	6 19
28¼	3 10	3 3	2 4½				Marishes Road	7 36	Sig.	1056	2 26		4 51				9 6	6 26
32	4 5	3 8	2 8				**Pickering 375**	7 45	1030	11 4	2 34		5 0				9 14	6 34
38	5 0	4 2	3 2				Levisham	7 58		1118	2 48		5 13				9 23	6 48
46½	6 3	5 2	3 10½				Goathland Mill	8 16		1136	3 6		5 31				9 46	7 6
50	6 7	5 6	4 2				Grosmont (See also page 375)	8 26		1146	3 16		5 40				9 56	7 16
53	7 2	6 0	4 5				Sleights	8 34		1154	3 24		5 48				10 4	7 24
54¼	7 3	6 1	4 6½				Ruswarp	8 39		1159	3 29		5 54				10 9	7 29
56	7 6	6 3	4 8				**Whitby 377** arr.	8 45		12 5	3 35		6 0	7b20			1015	7 35
—							**Malton** ....dep.	6 7	9 33	1036	1 53	3 4	4 23	5 21	5 53	7 4	8 43	5 58
25¼	3 6	2 11	2 1½				Rillington Junction	6 16	9 42		2 2		4 32		6 2		8 52	6 7
27¼	3 9	3 1	2 3½				Knapton	6 21	9 47		2 7		4 37		6 7		8 57	6 12
29½	4 0	3 4	2 5½				Heslerton	6 26	9 52		2 12		4 42		6 12		9 2	6 17
33	4 5	3 8	2 9				Weaverthorpe	6 32	10 0		2 20		4 50		6 20		9 10	6 25
34¾	4 8	3 11	2 10½				Ganton ....[below	6 36	10 4		2 24		4 54		6 24		9 14	6 29
39	5 4	4 5	3 3				Seamer Junc. 377 and	6 44	1013	11 5	2 33		5 3		6 33		9 23	6 38
45½	6 1	5 1	3 9½				Filey 377 ....arr.	8 45	1043	1139	2 54		5 30		8 19	8 19		
52½	7 0	5 10	4 4½				377 Bridlington .. "	9 11	1117	1213	3 30		6 2	6c50	8 57	8 57		
42	5 7	4 8	3 6				**Scarbro' 377** ....arr.	6 55	1025	1115	2 45	3 40	5 15	5 55	6 45	7 35	9 35	6 50

Miles	Single 1 cl. s. d.	Single 2 cl. s. d.	Single 3 cl. s. d.	Return 1 cl. s. d.	Return 2 cl. s. d.	Return 3 cl. s. d.	*From Whitby, p. 377.*	a	exp	mrn	mrn	mrn	exp	a	exp	a	exp	aft	Sndys aft
							Scarbro' ....dep.	6 45	8 20	9 20	1045		1 20	1 30	2 45	3 55	4 55	7 0	6 45
							377 Bridlington ..dep.		7 20	7f20	9 20			1239		2 41		5f45	
							Filey 377 .... "		7 57	7 57	9 52			1 14		3 19		6 13	
3	0 5	0 4	0 3				Seamer Junction	6 51	8 26	9 26				1 36		4 1		7 6	6 51
7½	1 1	0 10	0 7½				Ganton	7 0		9 35				1 45		4 10		7 15	7 0
9	1 4	1 1	0 9				Weaverthorpe	7 4		9 39	11 0			1 49		4 14		7 19	7 4
12¼	1 9	1 5	1 0½				Heslerton	7 11		9 47				1 56		4 22		7 26	7 12
14¼	2 0	1 8	1 2½				Knapton	7 16		9 52				2 1		4 27		7 31	7 17
16½	2 3	1 11	1 4½				Rillington Junction	7 21		9 57				2 5		4 32		7 36	7 22
21	2 10	2 4	1 9				**Malton 381, 375** ..arr.	7 30	8 50	10 7	1119		1 55	2 15	3 15	4 42	5 25	7 45	7 32
	From Whitby.						*Whitby Branch.* Mls												
							0 **Whitby** * dep.		6 45		9 20		1220			3 5		6 5	5 50
	0 3	0 2	0 1½				1½ Ruswarp		6 50		9 25		1225			3 10		6 10	5 55
	0 5	0 4	0 3				3 Sleights		6 55		9 30		1230			3 15		6 15	6 0
	0 11	0 9	0 6½				6¼ Grosmont (See also page 375)		7 3		9 38		1238			3 23		6 23	6 8
	1 4	1 1	0 9½				9½ Goathland Mill		7 13		9 48		1248			3 33		6 33	6 18
	2 6	2 1	1 6				18 Levisham		7 32		10 7		1 7			3 52		6 52	6 37
	3 2	2 8	2 0				24 **Pickering 375**		7 45		1020	1050	1 21			4 6		7 6	6 51
	3 9	3 1	2 3½				27¾ Marishes Road		7 53		d	1058	1 29			4 14		7 14	6 59
	4 0	3 4	2 6½				30¾ Rillington Junc.		8 0		d	11 3	1 36			4 21		7 21	7 6
	4 8	3 11	2 11				35 **Malton 381, 375** ar		8 9		1040	1112	1 45			4 30		7 30	7 15
	From Scarbro'.						56 Scarbro' ....arr.		9e0	e	1125		2 45			5 15		8e27	
—							**Malton** ....dep.	7 33	8 51	1010	1122		1 57	2 18	3 18	4 45	5 27	7 48	7 35
23½	3 2	2 8	1 11½				Huttons Ambo	7 39		1016				2 24		4 51		7 54	7 41
26	3 7	3 0	2 2				Castle Howard	7 45		1021				2 30		4 57		8 0	7 47
27	3 7	3 0	2 3				Kirkham Abbey	7 48		1025				2 33		5 0		8 3	7 50
30½	4 1	3 5	2 6½				Barton Hill	7 55		1034	1139			2 41		5 9		8 10	7 59
33	4 5	3 8	2 9				Flaxton	8 1		1040				2 47		5 15		8 16	8 5
35¾	4 9	4 0	2 11½				Strensall	8 7		1046				2 53		5 21		8 22	8 11
38	5 0	4 2	3 2				Haxby ..[381, 374, 361	8 12		1051				2 58		5 26		8 27	8 16
42	5 7	4 8	3 6				**York 200, 362, 367,** ar	8 25	9 27	11 5	1158		2 23	3 12	3 55	5 40	6 58	8 40	8 30
66¼	8 10	7 5	5 6¼				367 Normanton ....arr.	1048	1048	1210	1 25		3 48	5 5	5 5	7 15	7 15	1010	1010
67¼	9 0	7 6	5 7½				367 Leeds (New St.) "	1020	1020	1215	1 20		3 35	4 50	4 50	7 10	7 10	1020	1035

a Passengers for Whitby Branch change at Rillington. **b** Via Scarbro'. **c** Via Malton and Driffield. **d** Stops to take up for the Malton and Driffield and Malton and Thirsk Branches. **e** Via Forge Valley; Passengers not booked to or from Rillington and Marishes Road. **f** Leave at 8 30 mrn. and 6 5 aft. respectively for Malton and the South, via Driffield. * Town Station.

SCARBRO', SEAMER, and PICKERING.—North Eastern.

Mls	Fares 1 cl.	2 cl.	3 cl.	*From Hull, 377.*	mrn	mrn	aft	aft	aft
—				**Scarbro'** ....dep.	6 50	9 15	1 35	4 0	6 35
3	0 5	0 4	0 3	Seamer Junction	6 57	9 22	1 42	4 7	6 42
6¼	1 0	0 10	0 6¼	Forge Valley	7 7	9 32	1 52	4 17	6 52
8	1 1	0 11	0 8	Wykeham	7 11	9 36	1 56	4 21	6 56
9¼	1 4	1 2	0 9¼	Sawdon	7 15	9 40	2 0	4 25	7 0
11¼	1 7	1 4	0 11¼	Snainton	7 19	9 44	2 4	4 29	7 4
14	1 11	1 7	1 2	Wilton	7 25	9 50	2 10	4 35	7 10
16½	2 3	1 11	1 4½	Thornton Dale	7 31	9 56	2 16	4 41	7 16
20	2 8	2 3	1 8	**Pickering 375** ar	7 40	10 5	2 25	4 50	7 25

Mls	Fares 1 cl.	2 cl.	3 cl.	*Fm Helmsly, 375.*	mrn	mrn	aft	aft	aft
—				**Pickering** ...dep.	8 10	1035	2 45	5 20	7 37
3	0 6	0 5	0 3	Thornton Dale	8 18	1043	2 53	5 28	7 45
6	0 10	0 8	0 6	Wilton	8 21	1048	2 59	5 34	7 51
8¼	1 2	1 0	0 8¼	Snainton	8 30	1053	3 5	5 40	7 57
10	1 6	1 3	0 10	Sawdon	8 34	1058	3 9	5 44	8 1
12	1 7	1 4	1 0	Wykeham	8 38	11 3	3 13	5 48	8 5
13	1 11	1 7	1 1	Forge Valley	8 42	11 8	3 17	5 52	8 9
17	2 3	1 11	1 5	**Seamer Jun. 377**	8 50	1115	3 25	6 0	8 17
20	2 8	2 3	1 8	**Scarbro' 377** arr	9 0	1125	3 35	6 10	8 27

Bradshaws January 1891

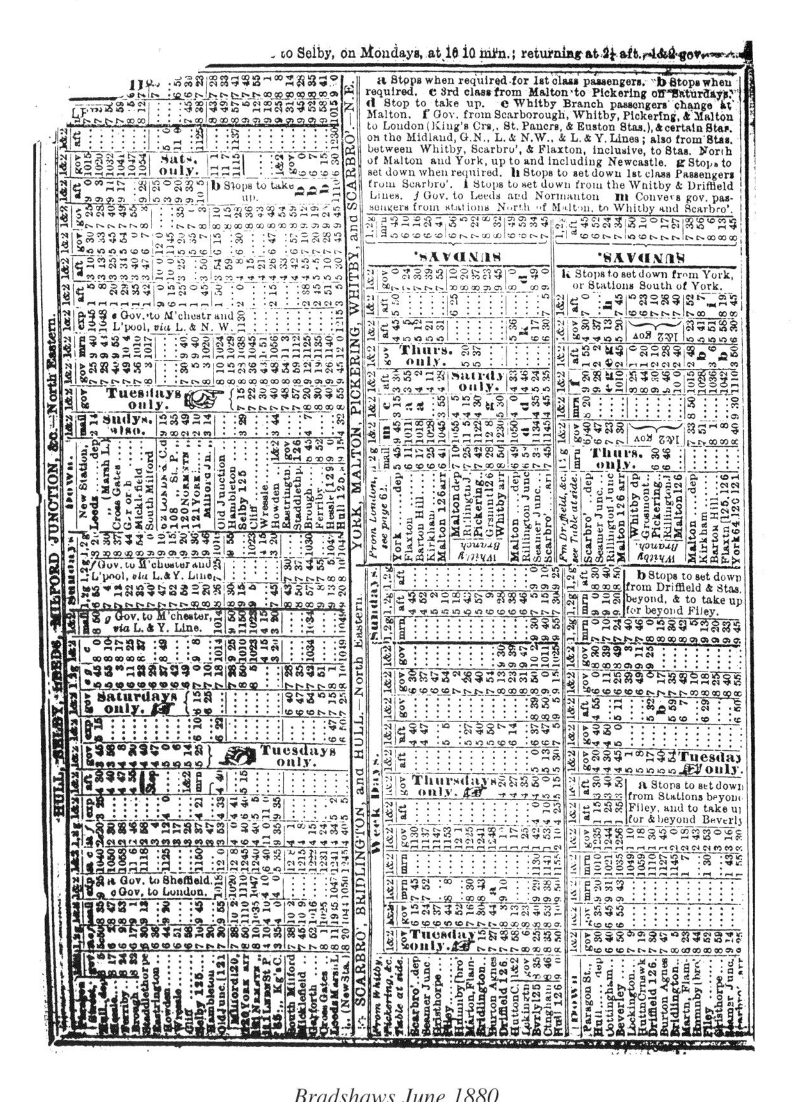

… to Selby, on Mondays, at 10 10 mrn.; returning at 2½ aft., 1&2 gov.

HULL, SELBY, LEEDS, MILFORD JUNCTION, &c.—North Eastern.

YORK, MALTON, PICKERING, WHITBY, and SCARBRO'.—N.E.

SCARBRO', BRIDLINGTON, and HULL.—North Eastern.

a Stops when required for 1st class passengers. b Stops when required. c 3rd class from Malton to Pickering on Saturdays. d Stop to take up. e Whitby Branch passengers change at Malton. f Gov. from Scarborough, Whitby, Pickering, & Malton to London (King's Crs., St. Pancrs, & Euston Stas.), & certain Stas. on the Midland, G.N., L. & N.W., & L. & Y. Lines; also from Stas. between Whitby, Scarbro', & Flaxton, inclusive, to Stas. North of Malton and York, up to and including Newcastle. g Stops to set down when required. h Stops to set down 1st class Passengers from Scarbro'. i Stops to set down from the Whitby & Driffield Lines. j Gov. to Leeds and Normanton m Conveys gov. passengers from stations North of Malton, to Whitby and Scarbro'.

k Stops to set down from York, or Stations South of York.

b Stops to set down from Driffield & Stas. beyond, & to take up for beyond Filey.

a Stops to set down from Stations beyond Filey, and to take up for & beyond Beverly.

a Gov. to Sheffield. c Gov. to London.

e Gov. to M'chestr and L'pool, via L. & N. W.

g Gov. to M'chester, via L. & Y. Line.

j Gov. to M'chester and L'pool, via L.&Y. Line.

Bradshaws June 1880

YORK, SCARBOROUGH, PICKERING, & WHITBY.—York and North Midland.

Fares from N'castle & Darlington to York, pp 70 & 71; from Leeds & Normanton to York, page 77.

Miles	Stations	Down 1 * 2 gov.	Down 1 2 3 mrn	Down 1 2 3 noon	Down 1 2 3 aft	Sundays 1 * 2 morn	Fares 1st s. d.	Fares 2nd s. d.	Fares 3rd s. d.
—	**York** ....dep.	7 0	..	12 0	5 30	7 † 0	..	..	..
4½	Haxby	7 7	..	12 7	5 37	7 7	1 0	0 9	0 6
6¾	Strensall	7 12	..	12 12	5 42	7 12	1 6	1 0	0 9
9½	Flaxton	7 20	..	12 19	5 48	7 20	2 0	1 6	1 0
11¾	Barton	7 25	..	12 25	5 55	7 25	2 6	2 0	1 6
15¼	Kirkham	7 35	..	12 35	6 5	7 35	3 6	2 6	2 0
16	Castle Howard	7 39	..	12 39	6 9	7 39	3 6	2 6	2 0
18½	Hutton	7 45	..	12 45	6 15	7 45	4 0	3 0	2 3
21¼	**Malton**	8 0	..	1 0	6 30	8 0	5 0	3 6	2 6
25¾	Rillington, Whitby J.	8 10	..	1 10	6 40	8 10	6 0	4 0	3 0
Whitby Branch. —	Rillingtn. for Wby.	8 10	10 3	1 20	6 40	8 0	..	..	..
29¼	Marishes Road	8 20	10 13	1 30	6 45	8 10	..	..	..
32¼	**Pickering**	8 35	10 30	1 40	7 0	8 30	8 0	5 6	4 0
38¼	Levisham	8 45	..	2 15	7 15	8 45	..	..	..
47¼	Goathland	9 15	..	2 50	7 45	9 15	..	..	..
50¼	Grosmont	9 40	..	3 10	8 0	9 40	..	..	..
53¼	Sleights	9 50	..	3 32	8 22	9 50	..	..	..
54¾	Ruswarp	9 55	..	3 40	8 25	9 55	..	..	..
56¼	**Whitby** ....arr.	10 0	..	3 45	8 30	10 0	12 0	9 6	7 0
37¾	Knapton	8 19	..	1 19	6 49	8 19	6 6	4 6	3 0
39½	Heslerton	8 23	..	1 23	6 53	8 23	6 6	4 6	3 6
33	Sherburn	8 32	..	1 32	7 2	8 32	7 6	5 6	4 0
34½	Ganton	8 36	..	1 36	7 6	8 36	8 0	5 6	4 0
38¾	Seamer	8 44	..	1 44	7 9	8 44	9 0	6 6	4 6
44¼	Filey	9 25	..	2 25	..	..	10 6	7 6	5 6
42¼	**Scarborough** arr	9 0	..	2 0	7 30	9 0	10 0	7 0	5 0

Miles	Stations	Up 1 2 3 mrn	Up 1 † 2 morn	Up 1 2 3 aft	Up 1 2 3 aft	Sundays 1 2 3 mrn	Sundays 1 * † 2 aft
—	**Scarborough**....dep	..	9 30	12 15	4* 5	..	4 5
9	Filey	..	..	10 50	3 51	..	..
3½	Seamer	..	9 44	12 25	4 15	..	4 15
7¾	Ganton	..	9 52	12 36	4 26	..	4 26
9¼	Sherburn	..	9 56	12 40	4 35	..	4 35
12¾	Heslerton	..	10 5	12 48	4 38	..	4 38
14½	Knapton	..	10 9	12 52	4 40	..	4 41
16½	Rillington, Whitby Junc.	..	10 18	1 0	4 50	..	4 50
Whitby Branch. 47	**Whitby** ......dep.	..	8 15	..	3 0	..	3 0
45½	Ruswarp	..	8 20	..	3 5	..	3 5
44	Sleights	..	8 25	..	3 10	..	3 10
41	Grosmont	..	8 35	..	3 20	..	3 20
38	Goathland	..	8 50	..	3 40	..	3 40
29	Levisham	..	9 25	..	4 5	..	4 5
23	**Pickering**	7 20	9 45	12 20	4 25	7 20	4 25
20	Marishes Road	7 30	9 55	12 35	4 35	7 30	4 35
16½	Rillington	7 50	10 5	12 50	4 50	7 40	4 50
21	**Malton**	..	10 30	1 10	5 0	..	5 0
23¾	Hutton	..	10 38	1 20	5 7	..	5 7
26¼	Castle Howard	..	10 45	1 25	5 12	..	5 12
27	Kirkham	..	10 48	1 30	5 15	..	5 15
30½	Barton	..	10 58	1 40	5 26	..	5 25
32¾	Flaxton	..	11 4	1 45	5 30	..	5 30
35½	Strensall	..	11 10	1 50	5 38	..	5 38
37¾	Haxby	..	11 15	1 56	5 43	..	5 43
42¼	**York**.........arr.	..	11 30	2 10	6 0	..	6 0

An omnibus for Castle Howard meets the trains at Castle Howard Station. Every York fortnightly fair a special train will leave Malton at 6 morn.

York to Thirsk, Darlington, & Newcastle, page 68. **To Leeds, Normanton, Wakefield, Halifax, and Manchester,** pages 77 and 89. * Mail trains. † Gov. trains.

TADCASTER, WETHERBY & HARROGATE.—York and North Midland. Supt., Charles Mason.

For trains from York to Church Fenton, page 79.

Mls. fm York.	Stations	Down 1 & 2 gov. morn	Down 1 2 3 class. morn	Down 1 2 3 class. morn	Fares from York 1st clss. s. d.	2nd clss. s. d.	3rd clss. s. d.	4th clss. s. d.
11	**Church Fenton** dep.	10 50	4 15	7 13	2 6	2 0	1 6	0 11
14½	Stutton	10 56	4 21	7 19	3 0	2 0	1 6	1 3
15½	Tadcaster	11 0	4 25	7 20	3 0	2 0	1 6	1 4
17½	Newton	11 5	4 30	7 26	..	..	..	..
19	Thorp Arch	11 10	4 35	7 33	3 6	2 6	2 0	1 7
21½	Wetherby	11 15	4 40	7 38	4 0	3 0	2 6	1 10
24½	**Spofforth**	11 25	4 50	7 50	4 0	3 0	2 6	2 1
72	**Harrogate** ......arr.	11 40	5 5	8 0	4 0	3 0	2 6	2 8

For trains from Church Fenton to Normanton, page 77.

Miles.	Stations	Up 1 2 gov. morn	Up 1 2 3 class. aft.	Up 1 2 3 class. aft.
—	**Harrogate** ....dep..	9 20	2 40	6 0
3	**Spofforth**	9 32	2 52	6 12
5½	Wetherby	9 37	3 2	6 17
8	Thorp Arch	9 44	3 7	6 24
9½	Newton	9 49	3 12	6 29
11½	Tadcaster	9 55	3 16	6 36
12½	Stutton	9 58	3 20	6 40
16½	**Church Fenton**....	10 15	3 25	6 46

Market Trains.—Tickets are issued on the Harrogate Branch by No. 1 train to York; to return by Nos. 2 & 3 trains from York. On Tuesdays a market train for Leeds will leave the Spofforth Station a 7 a.m. On Saturdays a train from Harrogate will reach York at 10½ a.m.

Church Fenton to Normanton, Derby, and London, page 77. **To York,** page 77.

Bradshaws March 1850

YORK, CASTLE HOWARD, MALTON, and SCARBOROUGH.—North Eastern.

Miles fm York	Down	mrn	mrn	mrn	mrn	mrn	mrn	mrn	aft	aft	aft	aft	aft	aft	aft	aft
	Central Station, 686 Newcastle ....dep.	1g57		m		8 0		1028		1230		1 44		2 40	3 54	5 4
	722 Leeds (New)... "	2 48		7 13		9 0	m	1155		2 0		4 13		5 25		6 0
	York ....dep.	4 25	5 43	8 13	9 12	10 0	1042	1245	1 0	2 42	3 40	5 3	5 7	6 3	6 30	6 55
4½	Haxby		5 52	8 22	9 20		1051		1 9		3 49		5 16		6 39	
6¾	Strensall		5 57	8 27	9 25		1056		1 14		3 54		5 21		6 44	
9½	Flaxton		6 3		9 31		11 2		1 20		4 1		5 27			
11¾	Barton Hill		6 9		9 36				1 26		4 7		5 33			7 13
15	Kirkham Abbey		6 16		9 43				1 33		4 15		5 40			
15¾	Castle Howard		6 19		9 46	1023			1 36		4 18		5 43			
18¾	Huttons Ambo		6 25		9 52				1 42		4 24		5 49			
21	Malton 720 ..... arr.	4 55	6 31		9 58	1032		1 14	1 48	3 11	4 30	5 31	5 55			7 29
	dep.	5 0	6 34		10 1	1036		1 17	1 51	3 14	4 33	5 35	5 58			7 32
25¼	Rillington		6 43		1010				2 0		4 42		6 7			
27½	Knapton		6 48		1015				2 5		4 47		6 12			
29¾	Heslerton		6 53		1020				2 10		4 52		6 17			
32¼	Weaverthorpe		7 0		1027				2 17		4 59		6 24			
34¼	Ganton		7 4		1031	d		1 34	2 21	3 32	5 3		6 28			
39	Seamer 705, 717		7 13		1040	11 4		1 42	2 30		5 12		6 38			
42	Scarborough 718..arr.	5 30	7 22		1049	1114		1 52	2 39	3 48	5 21	5 59	6 46	6 53		7 56

Down	aft	aft	Sundays mrn	Sundays mrn
Central Station, 686 Newcastle ...dep.		7 20	1 57	
722 Leeds (New)... "	7 2	9 25	2 48	9 0
York ....dep.	8 10	1035	5 5	9 57
Haxby	8 19	1044	5 15	
Strensall	8 24	1049	5 20	10 7
Flaxton	8 31		5 26	
Barton Hill	8 37		5 31	
Kirkham Abbey	8 45		5 40	
Castle Howard	8 48	c	5 43	1023
Huttons Ambo	8 54		5 49	
Malton 720 ..... arr.	9 0	1111	5 55	1033
dep.	9 3	1114	5 58	1037
Rillington	9 12		6 7	
Knapton	9 17		6 12	
Heslerton	9 22		6 17	
Weaverthorpe	9 29		6 25	
Ganton	9 33		6 29	
Seamer 705, 717	9 43		6 37	
Scarborough 718..arr.	9 51	1138	6 45	11 7

Up. — Week Days.

Miles	Up	mrn	mrn	mrn	mrn	mrn	mrn	mrn	aft	aft	aft	aft	aft	aft	aft
	Scarborough ......dep.	6 33		8 25	8 55	9 17		1035	1 17	1 30	2 40	4 5	4 55	5 55	
3	Seamer	6 40				9 24			1 24	1 37		4 12	5 2		
7¾	Ganton	6 48				9 32		1048		1 45	a	4 20	5 9		
9¾	Weaverthorpe	6 53				9 37		1053		1 50		4 25			
12¼	Heslerton	7 0				9 44				1 57		4 32			
14½	Knapton	7 5				9 49				2 2		4 37			
16¾	Rillington 720	7 10				9 54				2 7		4 42			
21	Malton 720 ..... arr.	7 18		8 49	9 19	10 2		1111	1 47	2 16	3 6	4 51	5 27		
	dep.	7 24		8 52	9 22	10 6		1115	1 50	2 18	3 9	4 54	5 28		
23¼	Huttons Ambo	7 30				1012				2 24		5 0			
26¼	Castle Howard	7 37				1017				2 29		5 5			
27	Kirkham Abbey	7 40				1021				2 32		5 8			
30¼	Barton Hill	7 49				1030	m	Sig.	b	2 40		5 15			
32½	Flaxton	7 56	m			1036	1110			2 46		5 21			
35¼	Strensall	8 2	8 35			1042	1116			2 52		5 27			6 55
37½	Haxby...[714,720,723	8 7	8 40			1047	1121			2 57		5 32			7 0
42	York 348, 684, arr.	8 21	8 53	9 20	9 50	11 0	1132	1149	2 22	3 10	3 37	5 45	5 58	6 45	7 13
67¼	723 Leeds (New)... arr.	9 5		10 0	1049	1218		1255	3 10		4 20		7 13	7 35	9 17
66½	684 Newcastle (C.) "			11 7	1155			2 45	5 3	5 25	6 42		7 55		1016

Up	aft	aft	aft	Sundays aft	Sundays aft
Scarborough ......dep.	7 0	8 0	10 0	6 45	8 5
Seamer	7 7			6 52	
Ganton	7 15			7 0	
Weaverthorpe	7 20			7 5	
Heslerton	7 27			7 13	
Knapton	7 32			7 18	
Rillington 720	7 37			7 23	
Malton 720 ..... arr.	7 45	8 28	1026	7 32	8 31
dep.	7 48	8 32	1029	7 35	8 36
Huttons Ambo	7 54			7 41	
Castle Howard	8 0			7 47	
Kirkham Abbey	8 3			7 50	
Barton Hill	8 10			7 59	
Flaxton	8 16			8 5	
Strensall	8 22			8 11	h
Haxby ..[714,720,723	8 27			8 16	
York 348, 684, arr.	8 40	9 2	11 0	8 30	9 6
723 Leeds (New)... arr.		9 56	1145		10 0
684 Newcastle (C.) "		1048	1h16		1151

NOTES.

- **a** Stops on Saturdays when required to take up for York and beyond.
- **b** Stops if required to take up.
- **c** Stops on Mondays when required to set down.
- **d** Stops if required to set down.
- *g* Leaves at 1 36 mrn. on Mondays.
- **h** Stops if required to set down from Scarborough.
- *h* Arrives at 2 58 mrn. on Sundays.
- **m** Auto-car.

☞ For other Trains

BETWEEN — PAGE
Malton and Rillington 720
Seamer and Scarborough 705, 716, 717

Bradshaws February 1910

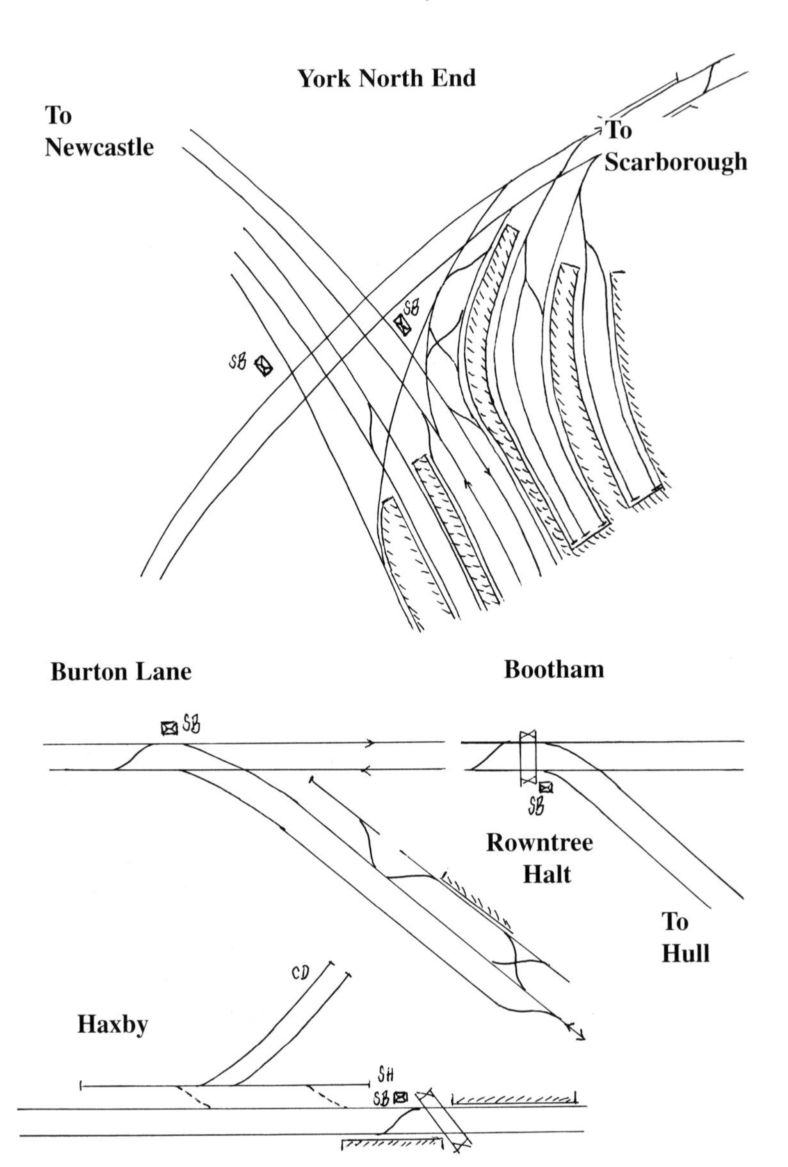
York North End
To Newcastle
To Scarborough
SB
SB
Burton Lane
SB
Bootham
SB
Rowntree Halt
To Hull
Haxby
CD
SH
SB

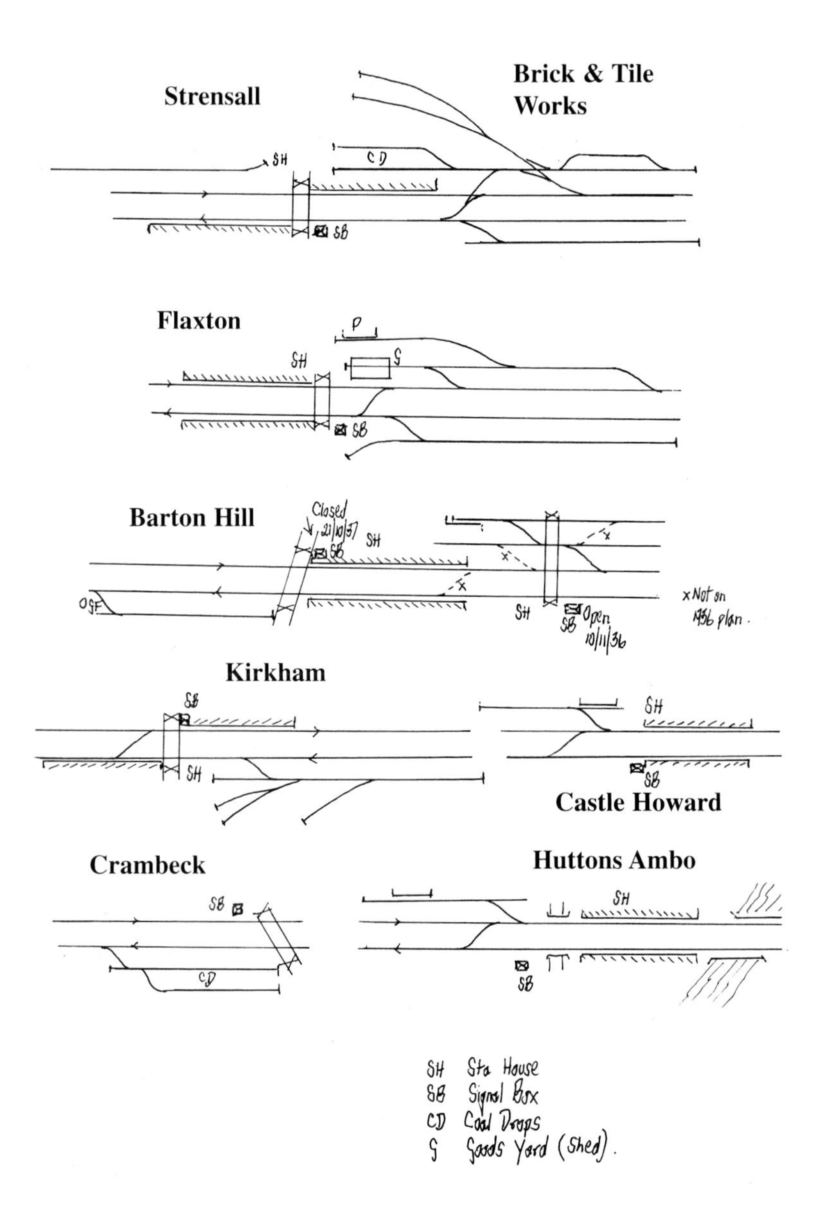

Strensall
Brick & Tile Works
SH
CD
SB
Flaxton
P
SH
G
SB
Barton Hill
Closed 21/10/37
SH
SB
OGF
SH
SB
Open 10/11/36
x Not on 1936 plan.
Kirkham
SB
SH
SH
SB
Castle Howard
Crambeck
SB
CD
Huttons Ambo
SH
SB
SH Sta House
SB Signal Box
CD Coal Drops
G Goods Yard (Shed).

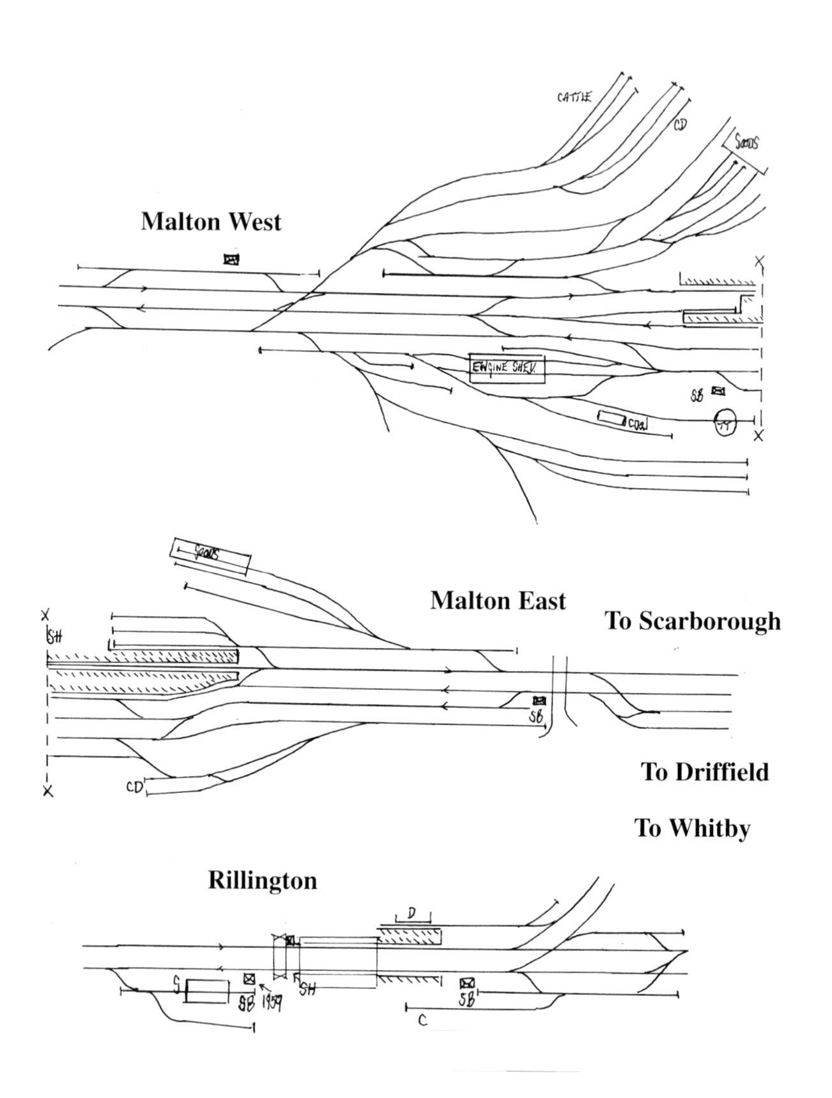

Malton West
CATTLE
CD
GOODS
ENGINE SHED
SB
COAL
GOODS
Malton East
To Scarborough
SH
SB
CD
To Driffield
To Whitby
Rillington
D
S
SB
1959
SH
SB
C

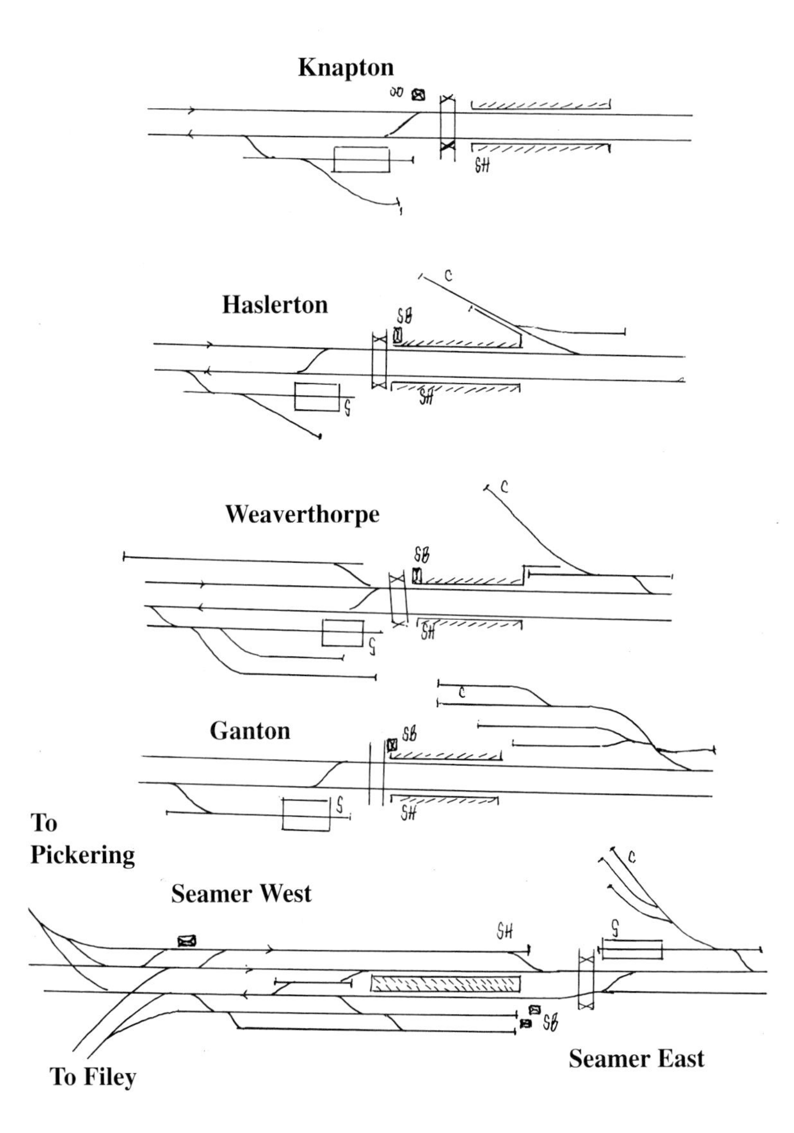
Knapton
SH
Haslerton
C
SB
S
SH
Weaverthorpe
C
SB
S
SH
C
Ganton
SB
S
SH
To Pickering
Seamer West
SH
C
S
SB
To Filey
Seamer East

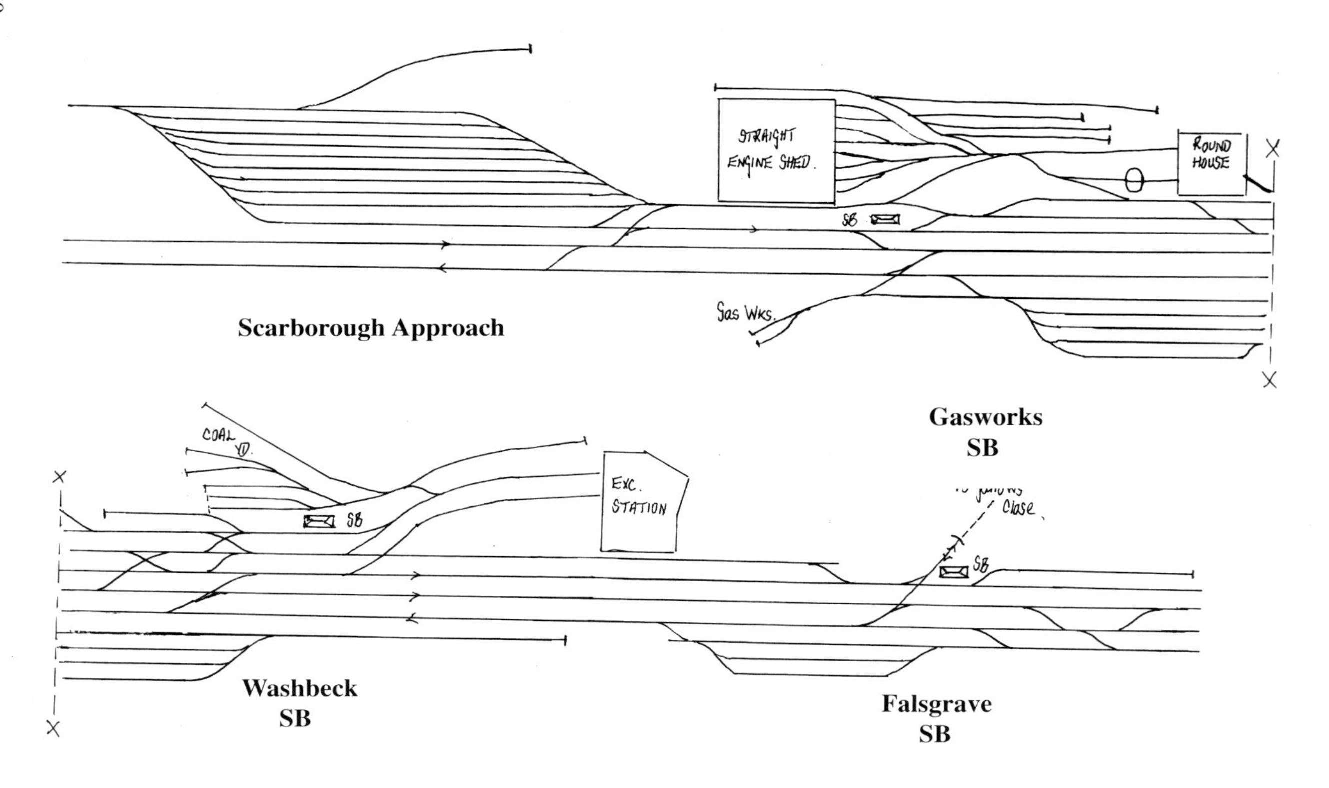

Scarborough Approach

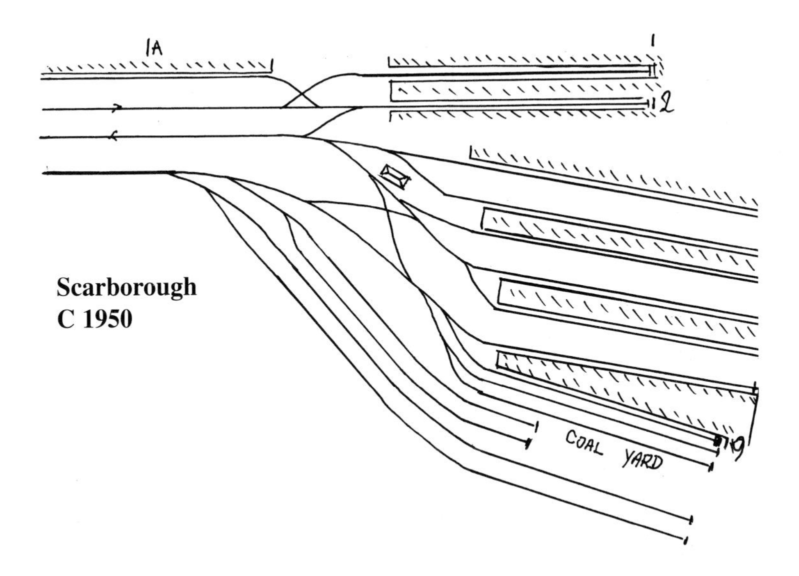

Scarborough
C 1950

Extracts from Special Workings Book
July 1925

SUNDAY, 12th JULY—continued.

No. **121.** **Leeds, York, Kirkham Abbey, Malton, Scarborough and Bridlington—Excursion.**

		a.m.			p.m.
Leeds	...dep.	8 35	Bridlington (c Scarbro')	dep.	7 35
Micklefield ...	...pass	8 55	Filey	...pass	8 0
Church Fenton ...	... ,,	9 5	Scarborough ...	...arr.	8 20
Copmanthorpe ...	...arr.	9 20	,, ...	...dep.	8 35
,, (c York)	...dep.	9 28	Malton	...arr.	9 8
York	...arr.	9 36	,, ...	...dep.	9 13
,, ...	...dep.	9 41	Kirkham Abbey ...	... ,,	9 25
Kirkham Abbey ...	... ,,	10 5	York (c York) ...	...arr.	9 50
Malton	...arr.	10 16	,, ...	...dep.	9 55
,, ...	...dep.	10 21	Church Fenton ...	...pass	10 12
Scarborough ...	...arr.	10 53	Micklefield ...	... ,,	10 22
,, (c Scarbro')	...dep.	11 10	Marsh Lane ...	...arr.	(c)10 38
Filey	...pass	11 27	,, ,, ...	...dep.	10 43
Bridlington ...	...arr.	11 52	Leeds	...arr.	10 46

Stock—1 XTLV (Fleece Inn), TS 2648 (Oatlands Inn), TS 3496 (Union Inn), TS 2692 (Prince of Wales Hotel), TS 2381 and 2379 (Newland Hotel) Leeds and Scarborough, 2 XTLV (Mr. Ellis' party), XTS 3756 (North West Ward Liberal Club) Leeds and Bridlington, 7 T, 1 B.

No. **103.** **Newcastle and Scarborough—Excursion.**

E.P.

		a.m.			p.m.
Newcastle... ...	...dep.	11 45	Scarborough ...	...dep.	7 45
Darlington ...	...arr.	12 37	Malton	...pass	8 13
,, ...	...dep.	12 42	York	...arr.	8 42
Northallerton ...	...pass	12 59	,, ...	...dep.	8 50
Thirsk	... ,,	1 8	Thirsk	...pass	9 17
York	...arr.	(c)1 34	Northallerton ...	... ,,	9 26
,, ...	...dep.	1 41	Darlington ...	...arr.	9 45
Malton	...pass	2 12	,, ...	...dep.	9 50
Scarborough ...	...arr.	2 40	Newcastle... ...	...arr.	10 42

For times between Newcastle and Darlington, see N.D. Programme.
Stock—5 XTLV, 2 XBLV.

No. **3.** **Nottingham to Scarborough—Troop Special.**

E.P.

		p.m.			p.m.
Doncaster... ...	...dep.	1 15	York	...dep.	(c)2 25
Shaftholme Jct. ...	...pass	1 22	Malton	...pass	3 0
Selby	... ,,	1 44	Scarborough ...	...arr.	3 35
York	...arr (z)	2 5			

Stock—G.N. Section (4 bogie vehicles, 9 21-ft. open trucks, 2 21-ft. covered trucks and 4 horse boxes, approximate weight 261½ tons).

Conveys South Notts. Hussars (12 officers, 210 men, guns, baggage and horses).

Empty train to return as soon as possible.

WEDNESDAY 15th JULY—continued.

No. **123.** **Leeds and Hull—Special Express.**

		a.m.
Neville Hill C. S.	...dep.	11t10
Leeds	...arr.	11t20
,, ...	...dep.	11 48
Micklefield ...	...pass	12 6
Gascoigne Wood	... ,,	12 12
Selby	... ,,	12 22
Staddlethorpe ...	... ,,	12 40
Hull	...arr.	(c) 1 3

		p.m.
Hull	...dep.	5 15
Staddlethorpe ...	...pass	5 37
Selby	... ,,	5 53
Gascoigne Wood	... ,,	6 2
Micklefield ...	... ,,	6 10
Cross Gates ...	...arr.	(c)6 20
,, ,, ...	...dep.	6·28
Leeds	...arr.	6 36
,, ...	...dep.	6t45
Neville Hill C. S.	...arr.	6t55

Stock—1 XOF, 2 XBFLV.

Conveys Society of Chemical Industry Party.

MALTON AGRICULTURAL SHOW.

No. **29.** **Scarborough and Malton—Stock Special "Q."**

		a.m.
Scarborough ...	...dep.	7 30
Heslerton ...	...arr.	7 53
,, ...	...dep.	8 0
Knapton	...arr.	8 5
,, ...	...dep.	8 10
Malton	...arr.	(c)8 20

Stock—1 B.

		p.m.
Malton	...dep.	5 50
Knapton	...arr.	6 0
,, ...	...dep.	6 10
Heslerton ...	...arr.	6 15
,, ...	...dep.	6 22
Seamer	...arr.	6 37
,, ...	...dep.	6 45
Scarborough ...	...arr.	(c)6 52

WEDNESDAY 15th JULY—continued.

No. **30.** **York and Malton.—Stock Special "Q."**

		a.m.			p.m.
York	...dep.	7 30	Malton	...dep.	7 20
Haxby	...arr.	7 39	Barton Hill ...	...arr.	7 38
,, ...	...dep.	7 47	,, ,, ...	...dep.	7 46
Strensall	...arr.	7 52	Flaxton	...arr.	7 52
,, ...	...dep.	7 57	,, ...	...dep.	7 58
Flaxton	...arr.	8 2	Strensall	...arr.	8 4
,, ...	...dep.	8 7	,, ...	...dep.	8 12
Barton Hill ...	...arr.	8 12	Haxby	...arr.	8 18
,, ,, ...	...dep.	8 17	,, ...	...dep.	8 23
Malton	...arr.	(c)8 35	York	...arr.	(c)8 33

Stock—1 B.

Freight Train Alteration.

8-35 a.m. D Goods York to Malton to leave at 9-5 a.m. and run correspondingly later throughout.

No. **185.** **Bridlington and Malton—Stock Special "Q."**

		a.m.			p.m.
Bridlington ...	...dep.	6 20	Malton	...dep.	6 0
Burton Agnes ...	...arr.	6 35	Scarborough Road Jct.	✠pass	6 3
,, ,, ...	...dep.	6 45	Wharram ...	✠arr.	6 12
Nafferton ...	...arr.	6 51	,, ...	⊕dep.	6 19
,, ...	...dep.	7 1	Burdale	⊕ ✠pass	6 23
Driffield	...arr.	7 5	Sledmere and Fimber	✠arr.	6 27
,, ...	...dep.	7 15	,, ,,	...dep.	6 34
,, West Jct.	✠arr.	7 17	Wetwang	...arr.	6 38
,, ,, ...	...dep.	7b57	,, ...	...dep.	6 45
Garton	...arr.	8 2	Garton	...arr.	6 51
,, ...	...dep.	8 11	,, ...	...dep.	6 59
Wetwang	...arr.	8 17	Driffield West ...	✠arr.	7 b 4
,, ...	...dep.	8 25	,, ,, ...	...dep.	7 18
Sledmere and Fimber	✠arr.	8 29	,, Station ...	...arr.	7 21
,, ,,	...dep.	8 37	,, ,, ...	...dep.	7 38
Burdale	⊕ ✠pass	8 43	Nafferton ...	...arr.	7 42
Wharram ...	⊕arr.	8 49	,, ...	...dep.	7 49
,, ...	✠dep.	8 59	Burton Agnes ...	...arr.	7 55
Scarborough Road Jct.	✠pass	9 10	,, ,, ...	...dep.	8 2
Malton	...arr.	(c)9 13	Bridlington ...	...arr.	8 15

Stock—1 B.

THURSDAY, 16th JULY—continued.

No. 77. Barnard Castle, Darlington, Thornaby, Middlesbrough, Redcar and Saltburn, returning to Middleton-in-Teesdale—Excursion.

		a.m.			p.m.
Barnard Castle ...	...dep.	8 52	Saltburn	...dep.	7 23
Darlington ...	...arr.	9 32	Redcar, Ex. Plat.	...arr.	7 35
,, ...	...dep.	9 39	,, ,, ,,	...dep.	7 38
Dinsdale	... ,,	9 48	Middlesbrough ...	...arr.	7 56
Eaglescliffe ...	...pass	9 56	,, ...	...dep.	7†58
Thornaby ...	...dep.	10 3	Thornaby ...	... ,,	8 5
Middlesbrough ...	...arr.	10 9	Eaglescliffe ...	...pass	8 12
,, ...	...dep.	10 11	Dinsdale	...dep.	8 22
Redcar, Excur. Plat.	...arr.	10 27	Darlington ...	...arr.	8 30
,, ,, ,,	...dep.	10 30	,, ...	...dep.	8 35
Saltburn	...arr.	10 42	Middleton-in-Teesdale	...arr.	9 45

† Precede 7-5 p.m. Parcels ex Saltburn.

For times Barnard Castle to Darlington and Darlington to Middleton-in-Teesdale, see N.D. Programme.

Stock—1 WT, 5 T, 2 B.

Bookings included from Richmond Branch to and from Darlington.

No. 1. York and Gilling—Empty Train.

Gilling and Scarborough—Day Excursion.

		a.m.			p.m.
York	...dep.	6t57	Scarborough ...	...dep.	7 30
Alne	...pass	7 15	Rillington... ...	... ,,	7 57
Sunbeck Jct. ...	⊕ ,,	7 25	Malton	...arr.	8 5
Coxwold	⊕ ,,	7 35	,, ...	...dep.	8 10
Gilling	⊕ ✠arr.	7t45	Scarborough Road Jct.	...arr.	8 13
,, ...	...dep.	8 1	,, ,,	⊕dep.	8 17
Hovingham Spa ...	... ,,	8 8	Amotherby ...	⊕ ,,	8 25
Slingsby	✠ ⊕ ,,	8 14	Barton-le-Street ...	... ,,	8 30
Barton-le-Street ...	... ,,	8 19	Slingsby	⊕ ✠ ,,	8 36
Amotherby ...	⊕ ,,	8 26	Hovingham Spa ...	... ,,	8 42
Scarborough Road Jct.	⊕arr.	8 33	Gilling	✠ ✠arr.	8 50
,, ,,	...dep.	8 37	,, ...	...dep.	9 t 0
Malton West Jct.	...arr.	8 41	Coxwold	⊕pass	9 10
,, ...	...dep.	8 55	Sunbeck Jct. ...	⊕ ,,	9 17
Rillington... ...	... ,,	9 3	Alne	... ,,	9‡25
Seamer ...	...arr. (c)	9 25	York	...arr.	10 t 2
,, ...	...dep.	9 29			
Scarborough ...	...arr.	9 35			

‡ Run on Slow line Alne to Tollerton and follow from there 8-5 p.m. E.P. and 8-16 p.m. Braked Perishable ex Newcastle.

Stock—12 T, 2 B.

A plan of levels between York and Scarborough

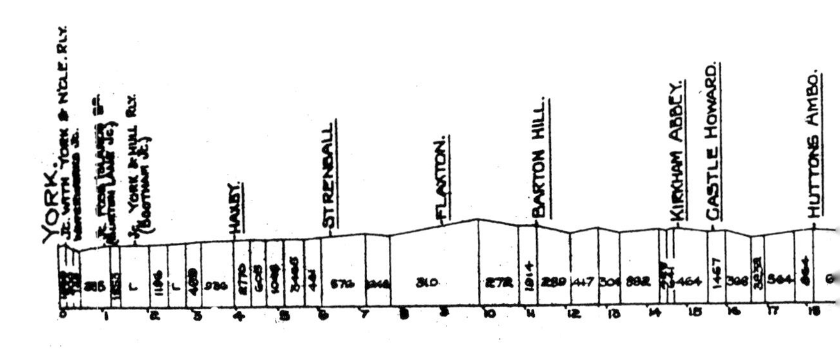

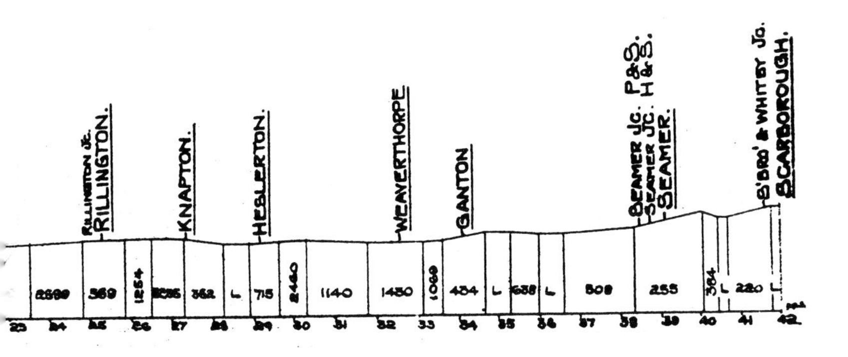
RILLINGTON JC.
RILLINGTON.
KNAPTON.
HESLERTON.
WEAVERTHORPE
GANTON
SEAMER JC. P&S.
SEAMER JC. H&S.
SEAMER.
S'BRO' & WHITBY JC.
SCARBOROUGH.
369
1254
362
L
715
2460
1140
1430
1069
434
L
L
508
255
384
L
220
L
23
24
25
26
27
28
29
30
31
32
33
34
35
36
37
38
39
40
41
42

Other publications by the the author:

'The Mexborough & Swinton Traction Company'.*

'The Burton & Ashby Light Railway'.

'Railways of South Yorkshire'.*

'Railways of North Lincs'.

'The Wakefield, Pontefract & Goole Railway'.

'The Railways of Castleford'.

'Huddersfield Branch Lines'.

'The Railways of Hull'.

'The Selby & Driffield Railway'.

'To the Crystal Palace'. (Forge Books)

'To the Alexandra Palace'. (Forge Books)

'Trentham, the Gardens and Branch Railway'.

'Doncaster's Trams & Trolleybuses'.

'The Dearne District Light Railways'.

'The Selby & Goole Railway'. (Oakwood)*

'The Wensleydale Branch'. (Oakwood)*

'The Hereford Loop'.(Oakwood)

'Railways of East Yorkshire'. (Oakwood)

(denotes those that are out of print but which may be in stock or available in libraries).*